The Murder of
Ivar Kreuger

By the same author

CARL MILLES

Teknisk Aktieanalys Del I
Teknisk Aktieanalys Del II
Teknisk Aktieanalys Del III
Teknisk Aktieanalys Del IV

Därför Mördades Ivar Kreuger
Kreuger-Mordet
Finanshajar och Imperiebyggare

Co-author

Ordbok för sekreterare
Ordbok för affärsfolk
Säljstrategier inför nästa börsras
Strategier inför nästa börsrally
Carlsson Trading Session

Co-author and translator

Cyklerna—Kretsloppen

Translator

Out of the inner Circle
Creating Excellence

Förlag: Decagon Research AB
Sandstensvägen 16, 167 64 Bromma, Sweden
Tel/Fax: 08-25 40 85; E-mail: *decagon.research@telia.com*

The Murder of Ivar Kreuger

The Mysterious Murder of
the Match King

Jonas Angstrom

To order additional copies of this book, contact:
Xlibris Corporation
1-888-795-4274
www.Xlibris.com
Orders@Xlibris.com
38867

CONTENTS

Should not the person be judged who like a parasite clings to the strong man, but when the strong man falls from his height, has not a word to say to his defense?

Foreword

The book "Why Ivar Kreuger was murdered" was published in 1990. Its contents became more extensive than originally planned, since I realized that I had to give explanations to a new generation, which was not familiar with the case of Ivar Kreuger. For that reason, I felt obligated to present a historical perspective, as well as to outline financial information and information of what happened after Ivar Kreuger's death.

No efforts had earlier been made to make a step by step analysis of the period around his death. No analysis of Kreuger's likely actions, in relation to his personality, had even been considered. There had not even been any contact with police or weapons experts. In addition there had been no concern or interest, in annotations made by the French police, or statements by medical examiners. Relative to these, I have discovered various cases of contradictory statements as questionable information, in various areas. This new information must now be analyzed and if possible, be proven and corrected.

Through the deciphering and analysis of radio telegrams, many of which were in codes, various earlier questions have been answered. Through analysis of the economical developments after 1932, by those who were most aggressive in the dismantling of the Kreuger Empire, sufficient facts and clues have allowed me to unearth and reveal the manipulations that actually took place. A very refined and in many cases impenetrable system which, both directly as well as indirectly, enabled the transfer of assets making them accessible, thereby enriching the caretakers, as well as their clients, was put into effect. Part of this story is presented in another chapter.

As the book "Why Ivar Kreuger was murdered" has so far only been printed in Swedish, I have elected to first make a condensed summary of it, in order to give the reader an overview of the specifics of the previous matters treated in the same. After that I shall follow up with newly discovered facts.

We will probably never be able to prove by 100 percent, how or by whom Ivar Kreuger was murdered, nor the intricate details of the dismemberment of his empire, since this would underestimate Kreuger's enemies. Throughout the years much material has been destroyed and assets have been moved around, in accordance with the purpose of letting time sweep away the footsteps. This has been done in a very skillful manner, but not with enough care, since then we would never have come as close to the truth as we are today.

We can still follow a chain of circumstantial evidence, which clearly points to the planned murder of Ivar Kreuger. His empire was wrecked, and his enemies stole its contents. Let us not forget that history has a tendency to repeat itself. Therefore, it is well worth the effort to review the case of Ivar Kreuger and the lies, which were created by his enemies, are still floating around, waiting for the truth to be revealed.

Introduction

Many books have been written on the fascinating subject—Ivar Kreuger and the Kreuger Empire. Surprisingly many authors have based their books on bad or in some cases even none existing source material. This is understandable when you learn that in Riksarkivet (the main Swedish government archive) all Kreuger related material (some 75 shelf meters) was classified as highly sensitive material, until the end of 1990, therefore requiring special permission from the Minister of Justice before it could be used for research. This requirement applied also to the archives kept by the Kriminalpolisen (Criminal police Dept.) as well. Many authors have not wanted to go through the troubles of getting the necessary permits; while especially family members were hindered from using the material in their research. Apart from the above-mentioned archives there is a telegram archive, which had previously gone unnoticed. Some of the telegrams (cables) are in code, which had to be deciphered, before the contents could be of any use. Considering the number and types of codes in existence, few authors have been willing to learn and to decipher them. In addition to the above, there are two large archives kept outside Sweden, which I hope to be able to go through some time in the not too distant future. Bank Director Holger Lauritzen (Director of Skandinaviska Kreditbolaget, Kreuger's bank contact in Sweden) followed Kreuger's business from 1919 until his death 1932 and kept notes on the more important transactions between Kreuger and the bank. After Ivar's death and on the advice of the Mayor of Stockholm, Mr.Lauritzen's notes were believed to have been destroyed. However, I have found a copy of these, being a most reliable source of information, since it concerns finances and was made by a prominent banker. This book, is therefore based on material from various archives, decoded telegrams and memory notes left by people who, themselves were engaged in and had considerable interest in the business of Ivar Kreuger, in one way or the another.

I will use quite a few quotations in this book, because I want to verify all specific statements made as far as possible. However, the quotations will not be translated with 100% accuracy, since our Swedish language has changed quite a bit since 1932. This would make true translation very awkward to read. At the end of a quotation, you will find one of the following abbreviations, making it possible to find the original quote, if that should be of interest.

RA= Riksarkivet (the Swedish National Archive); PA= Polisarkivet (the archives of the Swedish Criminal Police); SA= Stadsarkivet (the City archives); BA= Bolidenarkivet (the archive of Boliden Corporation); TK= Torsten Kreuger (the brother of Ivar); IK= Ivar Kreuger (himself); K&T= Kreuger & Toll (Ivar Kreuger's first corporation); SOA= Sven Olof Arleback(a Swedish Author); HL= Holger Lauritzen (director of Skandinaviska Kreditbolaget, a major Swedish Credit and Loan Banking Corporation); EB=Ernfrid Browaldh's archive (one of the administrators). Figures in brackets are reference numbers to my archive of photographed documents.

In my previous book, I mentioned that the Kreuger archive is difficult to work with and you get the feeling that things are arranged in a specific manner in order to show exactly just what is wanted to be shown. Most of the official Kreuger investigation was in fact made under these circumstances, as we will see later. It is obvious that documents have been taken from the archives and possibly destroyed. Sometimes, however, you find documents that you have been looking for in places where they should not be. They could be found among other files in a volume covering something completely different. Since the archives contain about 900 volumes (or subject matters), each one with an unknown number of files, this explains why the research is frustrating and time consuming.

In support of the above, it is interesting to note what the investigators and administrators themselves have written about the archive and the material it contains, whom I quote below.

The archive as such was turned over to the Riksarkivet on June 30th 1954 with the following reservation:
    "Considering the nature of the archive and the contents of the documents therein the administrators feel that the archive should not be open for research unless authorization is first given by the Minister of Justice or the Secretary of the Department of Justice; with the exception of other public authority, the administrators themselves and the Swedish Match Company, which could be interested in the books and documents, pertaining to the same."
(RA)

In June 1954, 22 years after Ivar's company Kreuger & Toll AB was declared bankrupt, the archive is considered to contain documents, of such sensitive nature that the archive remained under the "classified" lable, for more than another 40 years! Why?

There is more of interest to be learned from the Administrators and the Receivers in Bankruptcy. Let us find out what they say about the archive that they handled for so many years.

"At the beginning of the administration of the bankruptcy the administrators received a very large archive which was in an extremely bad state and partly mixed with the company's portfolio of commercial assets and securities. It contained contracts relative to bond issues and other written agreements of different nature and importance. It contained the companies and their managers' correspondence and a lot of other documents of various natures. To go through all this material and to sort it into different groups has been done through time and has required at lot of work. Special investigations were required frequently, in order to verify the contents of the documents and if they belonged to estates of others. Documents that did not belong to the Estate had to be separated and turned over to those companies to which they belonged such as STAB, IMCO's estate or IK's estate, a job that was complicated and could not be carried out, without controversy."

(Some of the documents, mostly IK's correspondence concerned several parties and a special agreement were made for them to be taken care of. With regard to IK's correspondence, kept on STAB's premises, controversy appeared and the administrators had to take action in order to be guaranteed free access, to this very important collection of letters, in order to guard the interest of the Estate.)

"Later—as the administration proceeded—and in such cases, where it had been possible to investigate the documents, the papers which seemed to lack importance have—after consideration by the administrators—been destroyed. A list covering destroyed papers have been made (Vol. 422) and with regard to other documents, such as participating debentures in store, forms for these, obligations etc., action was taken for a secure disposal. Altogether 80 sacks of such documents were destroyed. The control of this was effected by Lindeberg and Brolén, who also arranged and took care of the large archive that became the result of the bankruptcy administration."

Even if the text is very "heavy", there are interesting observations to be made, as follows:

— None of the investigators (with the possible exception of one, Mr. Prytz) had any knowledge or experience in international business. They were lawyers and bankers.
— As various types of codes were used in different business transactions, it is quite possible that important documents were among those, in the 80 sacks that were burned. A business letter written in code does not mean a thing to an outsider. As an example the purchase of 350,000 shares of Diamond Match Corp. was prepared through a number of letters in code. Of course these letters did not mention Diamond Match one single time. It was first when the transaction was concluded that an agreement was drawn in plain language
— Another interesting observation is that two of the administrators were also part of the Investigator Group, the same people who evidently made a mess of the archive from the beginning. This means that the administrators actually were criticizing themselves.

"The number of administrators were from the beginning five—three selected by Kungl. Maj:t (the Government) and two by the creditors. The number of administrators, decrease to two by the time the bankruptcy was about to be finalized. In addition there were people with lesser connection to the Administration; the liquidators of IK's estate, the liquidators for certain subsidiaries, persons replacing Kreuger & Toll's staff and the representative of the Court etc.

(RA)

"The following were administrators of the Estate of Kreuger & Toll:
Bank director Ernfrid Browaldh (1932), professor Martin Fehr (1932-1938), former Councilor of State Ernst Lyberg (1932-1933), J P Monnet (1932-1933), Assistant Justice of the Court of Appeal Sven Lindeberg (1932-1937), Bank director Nils Brolén (1932-1955), Judge Referee of the Supreme Court Hugo Ericsson (1933-1935), Bank director Léon Martin (1933-1955) and Auditor Sigurd R Wikland (1937-1945).

(RA)

Observe that both bank director Ernfrid Browaldh and Professor Martin Fehr were members of the special group of investigators who were called upon to *assist* the Board of Kreuger & Toll at the death of Ivar Kreuger. These investigators have frequently been named The Royal Commission. However, neither the King nor the Government in general, ever appointed any one of the investigators. This is a part of a huge bluff and misinformation.

There are two additional observations one can make from the introductory material at the Riksarkiv.
"The correspondence of Kreuger & Toll seems to have been handled from the later part of 1920 by the Investment Department", and that "Ivar Kreuger's private correspondence from about 1918/1919 is for the major part to be found in the archives of STAB."

(RA)

There is a note that tells us that also IK's correspondence was handled by the Investment Department of Kreuger & Toll.
The Investment Department of Kreuger & Toll seems to have handled all shares, bonds and debentures and this department also processed all mail and telegrams, as well; not only Kreuger & Toll's, but also the private correspondence of Ivar Kreuger. To be an insider—preferably with some influence—in this Department, must have been a very valuable asset. And this is exactly what somebody was blessed with.

The Kreuger Group of Companies/ the Kreuger Empire

The name of Ivar Kreuger is mostly connected with the match and he was called—and is still called—The King of Matches. Matches was only one of Kreuger's interests and I will try to give the reader a very compressed picture of the not so well known areas in which Kreuger was active. For those who want more detailed information I wish to refer to my previous book on the subject.

Kreuger's first company in Sweden—Kreuger & Toll—was founded together with Mr. Paul Toll in 1908. At that time Ivar Kreuger was 28 years old. The company was active as an entrepreneur in the building trade and had a very strong and fast growth. Kreuger had learned to build with reinforced concrete in the US and Kreuger & Toll was one of the first in Europe and definitely the first in Scandinavia to use this method[1]. In 1911 the company was turned into a joint stock company with a share capital of 1 million Swedish Crowns, which was a considerable amount at that time.

As the company grew it became quite natural to invest in companies related to the building trade. Thusly, Kreuger & Toll established a special company in Germany in order to keep an eye on that particular market. In Finland, Finska Kreuger & Toll and Betongbyggnads AB Tre Kronor were founded. In Sweden all properties were consolidated into the real estate Company—Fastighets AB Hufvudstaden.

The share capital of Kreuger & Toll was gradually increased to SEK 3 millions in 1916 with a capital reserve fund of SEK 1 million. Of the balance sheet total only SEK 416,000 represented outside capital; the remaining thusly being the company's own funds.

In 1917 the picture was radically changed, when the company became interested in match production. A new company was formed—Byggnads AB Kreuger & Toll—, which took over the building—and contracting business. The original Kreuger & Toll went into the field of financing and administration. This is also the first year that a holding of 60,000 shares, each at SEK 100:—, in the Swedish Match Company (STAB)

---

[1] IK obtain license to use the American Kahn method

appears on the balance sheet. In order to complete this transaction, the share capital was increased to SEK 6 million through the floating of a new issue of shares.

Let us take a closer look at the Swedish Match Company (STAB), since it was the match that made Ivar Kreuger internationally well known. How did Ivar Kreuger get into the field of matches?

In 1913 we find a great many match factories in Sweden—all being unprofitable. The banks, having provided the loans for these, were worried and began to look for someone, who could untangle the mess they had gotten themselvs into. After some time they found Ivar Kreuger[2], who, after serious negotiations, agreed to reconstruct the industry, according to a plan which he presented to the banks. This was the beginning of AB Förenade Tändstickfabrikerna (The United Match Companies). Through the fusion of the larger groups, the Swedish Match Company (STAB) was founded in December of 1917. STAB took over one of the larger group's—Jönköpingsgruppens—shares and inventoried them at the price paid. The United Match Companies' shares were also inventoried at the value they had, at the time of the fusion. STAB ended up with a share capital of SEK 45 million, with a reserve capital fund of a little more than SEK 61.7 million and with a balance sheet total of SEK 130 million. STAB became one of the largest companies in Sweden, already from the start. No write ups of values or good will were posted to the balance sheet.

During the years 1919-1920 STAB was consolidated and in 1920 Kreuger started to buy German match factories. During 1922 a new share issue was floated at the rate of 120% and the share capital was increased from SEK 45 million to SEK 90 million. The premium rate was added to the reserve capital, which increased to SEK 72 million. Of the issue, 40% was placed in England, through Higginson & Co, which company (through this transaction), carried out the first of many tasks, for the Kreuger Group. This was also the beginning of the internationalization of the financial division.

This may be the right place to quote bank director Holger Lauritzen's notes. Lauritzen was, as mentioned above, director of Skandinaviska Kreditaktiebolaget during 1919-1933 and followed closely Ivar Kreuger's and Kreuger& Tolls developments during these years. According to information the original of these notes were destroyed, upon the advice from the Mayor of Stockholm.[3]

---

[2]   IK's father and uncle had two small match factories. Thus IK was familiar with the problems.

[3]   However, through my research I have been able to recover a copy. These notes are considered to be very valuable as source material as the author himself observed and took part in many of the important episodes.

I will quote Lauritzen for some of the periods and episodes during the development of Kreuger & Toll and the career of Ivar Kreuger:

"In the middle or possibly in the end of 1919 a consortium was formed consisting of on one hand Ivar Kreuger and on the other hand AB Kreuger & Toll, Centralgruppens Emissionsbolag, Aktiebolaget Fortitudo, Aktiebolaget Handion and Svenska Emissionsbolaget (companies belonging to the Swedish banks), on the other. In order to protect STAB's interests from the competition of foreign countries, caused by the currency situation, Kreuger had already begun to acquire certain foreign match companies. He had at an early stage come to the conclusion that acquisitions must be made on a larger scale, but that it was not suitable that such acquisitions be made by STAB. He suggested that a special organization should be formed for this purpose. The suggestion was made to Svenska Handelsbanken and Skandinaviska Kredit AB. The consortium should have to its disposal a capital of up to SEK 60 million. This capital should be held at disposal by the banks against Kreuger's notes and with security in the shares, of the companies acquired together with the guarantees of the other members of the consortium. The acquisitions should be made according to Kreuger's instructions but any two members of the consortium should have veto.

The financing should be made on 50/50 bases between the two banks. The agreement should be made for a period of five years. I was present at a meeting in Emissionsbolaget at which also bank director Frisk, the directors of Emissionsbolaget, Aron Andersson and Thunberg were present and it is possible that the bank directors Mauritz Philipson, Lettström and Rydbeck, also were present. I remember how I expressed roughly something like the following: "The business seems to me to be a little risky, as it completely depends on one person even if it has been said that STAB in the future will acquire all the assets. But there ought to be a "blasting/busting clause" to the advantage of the members of the consortium, as this will be a long time business." That was when Andersson took me to the side and told me that I apparently did not know that Kreuger was enormously rich and that STAB yearly could put aside many millions in order to bring together the amounts needed for the final take over.

Kreuger, himself declared that my point of view was correct and a clause was added to the agreement to the fact, that when two partners in the consortium so wished, the consortium should be dissolved, with the obligation for Kreuger to acquire the portions belonging to the other members. It is quite possible that Kreuger also had the right to do the same thing, if and when he so wished. During the time that followed, foreign match companies were bought up to an amount of SEK 50 million. These acquisitions were financed, as agreed by the banks, with SEK 25 million each.

Jonas Angstrom

In the end of October 1921 I went to America on business for Skandinaviska Banken and traveled at the same time as Kreuger. At this time, the, so-called, "Peace Crisis", had begun.

In New York, I met Kreuger frequently. Wherever I came in New York, I realized that people knew Ivar Kreuger and thought highly of him. When I was with the Morgan Group to which I got an introduction from the New York Trust Company, I met Morgan, Lamont and Stettinius. Stettinius had been the president of Diamond Match Company and had had a prominent position in the War Department, during the war. He was the one, in the Morgan Group that I talked to most of the time. Among other things he said: "You have a good man in Sweden, in Ivar Kreuger. This is really something for you to pay attention to and take care of."

At this time there was also a group from Japan, which Kreuger was negotiating with, regarding some match factories in Japan. Kreugers main interest, at that time, was to establish an organization in New York, which could serve as a hub for foreign match holdings. A little later, this took the form of International Match Corporation. I became strongly impressed, by the overpowering and important role Kreuger played in America. One of the first days after my return to Sweden, I met with Admiral Lidman, who was the chairman of Handelsbanken. He was worried about the business of the Consortium and was interested to hear my impressions of my trip. I told him: "We do not need to be worried about the Consortium. Here in Sweden we do not know what connections and what a position Kreuger has in America." I said the same thing to the bank inspector.

Financial times became worse, however, and at a point at the end of 1922, I told Kreuger that it was necessary to ease the Consortiums engagements as soon as possible and arrange it, so that STAB could take care of the business. Kreuger replied that he did not think that the time was ripe just yet, but after another reminder he promised to discuss the matter with the Board of STAB.

A meeting was thereafter held at STAB, where I was present, although I was not a member of the Board. Kreuger presented, and outlined the business of the Consortium and made an offer to STAB, to take over. It was agreed that certain assets were to be taken over by STAB and that STAB accepted some of the Consortium's obligations. STAB also declared that it, in principle, was willing to take over the whole business at a later date. After this agreement, the banks considered their engagements with STAB, to be free of risks. In October 1924, Ivar Kreuger took over shares in the Consortium, which belonged to the subsidiary companies of the banks. A little later he turned over all the assets to the company, he had formed under the name of International Match Corporation, which shares, in turn, were taken over by STAB.

This complete business transaction is an example of Kreuger's way to acquire large objects, which he at a later date, when he found the time to be right, turned over to one or another company within the Kreuger Group. The 50,000 shares in Grängesberg, which were bought from us in 1927, were also bought by Kreuger himself, but in which company they ended up—I do not know. However, it was with Ivar Kreuger himself, that we closed the deal."

One interesting part of Holger Lauritzen's notes is that the draft is dated in June 1934, but this date has been crossed over and replaced with 1935. The notes were written a few years after Ivar Kreuger's death at a time when very many people had "changed their minds" about him. When Lauritzen wrote this summary there were no reasons for him to be other than neutral, that is to say things as they were and as he remembered them. I can very well understand that he was advised to destroy his notes, as they did not completely agree with the opinion of Ivar Kreuger, which his opponents had decided should prevail. We can, at any rate, consider him as a first hand witness, from that time.

International Match Company (IMC) was formed during 1923. This was a natural and necessary step as the match business and other transactions, outside Sweden, became the larger part of the Kreuger Group's activities. It was to the US the Group had to turn in order to get financing. However, in order to be able to keep full control over the various companies (directly or indirectly), it was necessary to build a chain of companies, that very often came to own each other, cross wise.

STAB acquired a little more than 50% of the shares in IMCO and used the main part of their foreign match interests as payment. At the same time, when IMCO was formed, a $15 million bond issue was released at 6.5%. The forming of IMCO provided the Kreuger Group with roughly $30 million and it is worth noting that the Rockefeller name was on the subscription list. Other news of interest is that IMCO bought Rockefeller's match interests in Canada and paid with their own shares.

During 1924 two larger issues were introduced to the market. These represented an inovation, being a new Ivar Kreuger creation—the B-share—which he introduced on the world market for the first time. The STAB B-share had in this particular case 1/1000 of a voting right. It was Higgins on & Co that floated the major part of the first issue, of 900,000 B-shares, on the London Stock Exchange. The second issue, shares in IMCO, was floated, in order to redeem the bonds. In reality, this represented a conversion.

In England British Match was formed, with STAB holding 30% of the capital, which amounted to £6 million, resulting in STAB's domination of the match production in the British Empire. In Japan, Daido Match Co. was formed through a fusion of the country's most important match factories.

Apart from acquisitions and mergers of existing match factories in different countries, STAB was also in the position to negotiate, either for the total match production, or just for the marketing of matches. This was of course made easier, if it was connected with a loan to the Government in question, at a favorable rate of interest, collateralized by a Government bond issue. At the death of Ivar, the Kreuger Group controlled roughly 85% of the world market for matches. Having reached this powerful position the Group had also become "dangerous" to others.

The match, in itself, was a product of necessity, which in a way made it insensitive to the Market and it's general business cycle. When the Group's system (network) was fully expanded, it would practically always be in a state of full liquidity. Loans in connection with a monopoly could be made interesting, from an interest point of view and could also, to a certain degree, be made "self repaying". However, this was not to the liking of some of the world's banking interests. Even if monopolies, for the production of matches, could be accepted, there was the risk that the same system would be applied to other products, on the various markets, where the Kreuger Group was active or intended to become active. As something of a by-product, business transactions in stocks, bonds, debentures and other securities of various types, became a growing part of the Group's activities. The larger the Group became, the more these activities increased. For some of the world's private bankers, banking houses and other financial institutions, this was life threatening. This was competition, which could not be accepted.

STAB was the Group's largest single interest and it was growing. It was, however, first during the period 1925-1930 that the various business deals became a bit entangled. The reason for this was that during this period, the large monopolies for matches, the Government loans and the bond and share issues originated. However, the Group had many other fields of interest.

Real Estate

The real estate holding company—Fastighets Aktiebolaget Hufvudstaden (Hufvudstaden—meaning Capital City)—was founded in 1915 with a share capital of SEK 600,000-1,800,000, whereof SEK 200,000 was taken over by K&T. At that time it owned five houses. Year after year the company added new houses to its holdings and in 1924 it was the owner of 24 buildings, with a book value of SEK 12,4 million. In 1929 it had become the largest Real Estate Company in Sweden. Apart from Hufvudstaden, Kreuger & Toll owned buildings in Germany and France and in some other countries, where the Group had interests of one type or another. How all these properties were administrated, after the death of Ivar Kreuger is quite an interesting story which has its place, and will be presented, in a coming book.

AB Svensk Filmindustri (The Swedish Movie Industry)

This company was acquired in 1919 and in 1920 had assets in the balance sheet, composed of it's 30,000 shares at SEK 20:—each, or a book value of SEK 600,000:-. It is interesting reading to follow this company during the "reconstruction" and bankruptcy of Kreuger & Toll, after Ivar Kreuger's death, and see how it ended up in the hands of Bonnier[5].

Mining interests

Apart from Grängesberg in Sweden, Kreuger & Toll had interests in Algeria, Morocco and in Algarrobo in Chile. Through these and other holdings a little more than 17% of all iron ore, worth mining, in the world was controlled. Negotiations were also in the process for the acquisition of the deposits at Wabana, Newfoundland. In this particular case, there are indications of a potential partner in the Rockefeller group, on one side and increasing risks for controversies with Morgan (Jr.), on another front.

Wood, paper, pulp and cellulose

Svenska Cellulosa Aktiebolaget, was formed, and Kreuger & Toll acquired the entire share capital, with the exception of the 4 founders' shares. SCA became the largest wood, paper—and powercompany in Europé, with forestland of 1,6 million hectare, among other assets. During his last months in New York, Kreuger was negotiating the possibilities of discounting or, in some other way, to finance the credits that SCA received, when exporting its products. He was not only doing this for SCA, but also for the rest of the Swedish forest industry.

Bank interests

Kreuger & Toll had, for obvious reasons, interests in Skandinaviska Kredit Aktiebolaget (Skandbanken) and Stockholms Intecknings-Garanti Aktiebolag (mortgage bank), but apart from these holding it owned large blocks of shares of Svenska Handelsbanken, Smålands Banken, Östgötabanken, Sundsvallsbanken and a smaller block in Vänersborgsbanken. Outside of Sweden the Kreuger Group had interests in private banks, as well as banks, such as Deutsche Union Bank etc.

---

[5]   The Bonnier family were owners of the Dagens Nyheter (DN) and its head was on the board of directors of Enskilda Banken

Minority interests

The Kreuger Group also had and had had large interests in companies such as SKF, Stora Kopparberg, Kopparfors, Separator, Fläkt, Bergvik-Ala, Telefonos de Mexico (in Mexico), as well as in US Steel and General Electric. There were also considerable holdings in the German Young and Kreuger loans, as well as Government bonds from Hungary, Rumania, Yugoslavia, Greece, Italy and French rentés.

The Boliden Mine

The mine, with complex deposits of copper, zinc, silver and gold, was one of the richest (if not the richest) mine in Europe. During his last months in New York Ivar Kreuger was negotiating a deal with the Guggenheims's of New York, who were interested in some participation, which might have solved the liquidity crises of Kreuger & Toll for some time. Kreuger was, however, not in a hurry and more about Boliden will follow, in a chapter further on in this book.

Kreuger & Toll's as well as International Match Corporation's books were audited by the wellknown American firm of Certified accountants Ernst & Ernst appointed by Lee, Higginson & Co, USA. In Sweden qualified Swedish accountants checked all accounts and books on a day to day basis. One important question must be raised: "Is it possible that none of these auditors during all of these years should not have discovered the errors or inconsistencies in the books, if there was (or had been) anything wrong?"

The Fiscal Balance of Kreuger & Toll, as of December 31, 1931 was, SEK 1,247'537,216:11.

Did the Real Estate company Hufvudstaden, with all its buildings in Sweden, the houses in Berlin and Paris; SCA with its vast forest area; Grängesberg and Boliden with their ore deposits; STAB with all its match factories and monopolies not exist? Had the various Governments that issued their Bonds and permitted the monopolies not received their loans?

Yes, everything was there but, in spite of this was Kreuger & Toll, with its more than 160 companies, declared to be a bluff; thin air and fraud. And this—dear reader—was declared after less than 2 months, following the murder of Ivar Kreuger.

Did the banks or other lenders loose anything? No, of course not! They got their capital, their interest, their service costs and whatever they could dream up to 100%. As usual, it was the little guy who lost everything he had invested.

Annotation

In this book, I am presenting the financial situation, as it was at the end of 1931 and later. It should be remembered that, in the end of the month of September of 1931, the Swedish Crown dropped almost instantaneously by 30% in its value against the dollar and similarly against the German Mark and French Francs. Sweden discontinued the use of the Gold Standard, as the backup standard for the Crown. This caused the Crown to enter a "floating" state, for some time until it regained stability. During this time, especially, it was easy for smart and knowledgeable people to make the public believe things that were not true. Fluctuations were broad, to begin with, as is always the case, when currency reform is in the making.

The Crown's 30% drop against the dollar, didn't hurt or decrease the strenght of the Kreuger Group. The actual value (at home in Sweden) had an almost instantaneous appreciation of the 30%, which is not mentioned anywhere and thusly was hidden for the people. Since the majority of the assets of the Group were outside of Sweden, the Group continued (in it's fragmented state—after the vultures divided it), as it had before. There was no increased adverse effect on the individual companies by the "World Situation", as it existed, but the average Swede lost real value. The banks foreclosed on him, with the devaluation as a pretext. The Depression had started about three (3) years earlier, but the Group was in good condition, due to its international characteristics.

As is thusly seen, the main effect of the removal of the Gold Standard was a "temporary inconvenience", but it was used by banks and others as a tool to improve their personal situation, rather than permanent damage (except for the damage they caused the small individual investor).

Why was Ivar Kreuger killed?

You can not build a financial empire and an organization of the size of the Kreuger Group, without creating hurt feelings in others, whether you like it or not. Kreuger had, as far as I can see, three basic blocks of opponents: The communistic block with Russia as one main party; The World Bankers represented by J P Morgan, and the Wallenberg Group in Sweden. You could, possibly, cut down the numbers to two (2), since Morgan and Wallenberg could possibly be linked together and counted as one Group, for the purposes of the present.

Ivar Kreuger[6] tried to do business with the communists in Russia in the middle of the 1920th, but his conditions;—that they paid Russia's old debts—could not be accepted, for which reasons the negotiations broke down. The large loans to France and Germany, that Kreuger arranged, were intended to stabilize the European economy. At that time this was far from the desires of Russia. When the Kreuger Group continued with their loans for stabilizing, in exchange for market advantages, within these countries, they unknowingly created, what more-or-less became a disaster. The very foundation for the Communists political system became endangered. Kreuger & Toll built something of a psycological trading fence around Russia and orders, for Russian matches were withdrawn. This made it mandatory for Stalin, to declare that Ivar Kreuger should be considered an enemy of Russia, and enemies should be taken care of, using any and all means that could be found.

From IK's diary in 1926 the following notes can be read:
Feb 22, The Russian contract
April 27 Russian discussions
Sept 22 Per Albin Hansson[7]

In IK's diary from September 11th 1931 you can read the following notes:
Person
Soviet 20 blackmail paper
15,000,000
Grönberg 4 pm

---

[6]   Prior to the revolution Kreuger had made investments in Russia, and had owned some small plants and businesses.

[7]   after IK's death in 1932 P A Hansson became Prime Minister for the social democrats

The Murder of Ivar Kreuger

These extracts are type written copies found in the police archive in Stockholm. No explanation has been available.

If one studies the international politics from that time, one will find that the communists were not happy at all with the activities of Kreuger & Toll. What actions could and should they take, in order to remove Ivar Kreuger from the financial stage? Because, he `had to be´ removed.

The world banker Morgan's net of international contacts was well known. He could not stand competition, nor that anybody became so big, that he could disrupt Morgan's sphere of power. It was during the second part of the 1920th that the foundation was laid for the big and more serious conflicts, between the Morgan and the Kreuger Groups. It began when Morgan attempted to press France for an 8 % interest loan, which he was quite sure that only he would be able to arrange. Kreuger went ahead and lent France the same amount, but at the rate of 5%, with the result that some sales advantages for STAB, became included as well. Several similar loan transactions followed and Kreuger also supported the stabilization of the German economy, in a way, which was not in accordance with Morgans thinking of how the economy should have been arranged.

Kreuger's interests in LM Ericsson and the possibility for him to get telephone monopolies in those countries, where his Group already had monopolies on matches (or somehow covered the market in another way), was definitely a threat to Morgans interests in ITT. Signs could also be that Kreuger was on his way into areas, which would disturb Morgans interests in steel and Kreuger's connection with Rockefeller, could also lead to serious effects in other areas—such as petroleum.

Kreuger had to be stopped. But how?
During the stock market crash, starting in 1928, there were strong indications of considerable short selling of various issues, by financial institutions, followed by a severe shortening of credit. The crisis deepened and was amplified by deliberate inactivity, on the Credit Market. New loans were not accepted and the collateral for old loans had to be increased. Down payments also had to be increased and in some cases, even the whole loan had to be repaid.

It is said that the Morgan Group "was thriving like a fish in the water". They earned big amounts on bankruptcies and short selling. Big profits could be made, by shorting Kreuger securities, and it is well known that very large amounts of these were sold in New York. In fact, a great many more were sold than had ever been issued. Forged deposit certificates and "blocked" collateral were sold. Short selling did not only take place in New York, but also in Paris and Amsterdam, as well as in Stockholm (as we will see a little further on) and Ivar Kreuger knew, to a certain extent, who was behind them all. The time for settlement, of the sales, came closer and together with that catastrophe. If the delivery of the certificates, which were sold, could not take place or the forged certificates could not be replaced with genuine ones, there would be disaster. The situation was precarious for quite a few brokers, especially in Paris. Some of these brokers had been dealing for (and with) Swedish clients and accounts.

(Swedish authorities at all levels have denied that Ivar Kreuger and the Kreuger Group had been slandered and had been subject to criminal short selling of among other things forged debentures and certificates of deposit. In a while I will prove that these denials are false).

The business deals of the Wallenberg sphere—being Swedens largest and most prestigious private banking group with international contacts—had been numerous prior to 1932, although not always of the "best" kind. Increasingly, its endeavors were pushed into the financial background, with a few exceptions. No industries were created or expanded. Banking was the main business together with trading of securities, administration, and bankruptcies that were not always on a 100% level of cleanliness.

Ivar Kreuger received enormous attention. He built and created—built in a new way. He merged and created large industries. He borrowed and lent money and invested many times in companies that the Wallenberg Group for one reason or the other had wanted to put their hands on. It is in connection with transactions of this sort that Kreuger comes on a collision course with the Wallenberg's. There is no doubt what so ever that Kreuger proved to be a veritable challenge for the Wallenberg Group. When, for instance, Wallenberg was approached by a foreign company, that had shown interest in the Boliden mine, they were not invited to the negotiation table—all negotiations were held with Ivar Kreuger. Neither should Kreuger's rather large interests in other banks be forgotten. The day that he might decide to do something in the banking business the general situation could become very serious for the Wallenberg's.

In Sweden, people would doubt this statement, based upon the Wallenberg group's present power sphere. But it is enough to take one look at what the Wallenberg/SEB (SEB= Stockholms Enskilda Bank) combine was prior to 1932, and how the picture was changed, when they began to administer the fundamentally sound Kreuger companies that were taken over in connection with the bankruptcy of Kreuger & Toll.

Other groups could also have had an interest in the disappearance of Ivar Kreuger. However, we will focus on those mentioned above, as they still can be traced to a large extent. Not in a way, that you can put your finger on this or that person, or this or that group of persons. Because their work was in the planning. Services are bought. Even planning can be bought. Such things have happened throughout history—and, it still happens today. Nothing is new under the sun.

Who or whom gained the most from the death of Ivar Kreuger? According to Swedish and international opinion they were the Morgan Group and the Wallenberg Group. (A detailed description of the above mentioned Groups is outlined in my previous book "Därför Mördades Ivar Kreuger (Why Ivar Kreuger was murdered)).

Kreuger and the Jews

A claim has been made that a Jewish syndicate was attacking the Kreuger Group. There have also been claims that Kreuger himself was a Jew or had Jewish ancestors. I have been unable to trace the origin of these statements. However, the statements incorrectness can be clearly seen from the genealogy work of E. E. Areen, which goes back six generations. According to this work Ivar Kreuger was of a pure Teutonic race. Of his ancestors 78 were born in Sweden, whereof 71 in the province of Småland.

In some cases it has been claimed that Kreuger hated Jews, but as far as my research has revealed, this is not true at all. There is nothing in the more serious literature that indicates that this could be the case.

Personally, I do not believe that Kreuger was the sort of person that could hate someone—no matter what race. Dislike maybe, but not hate. There is one note made about a statement that Ivar Kreuger should have made with regard to Jews: "There are two sorts of Jews, those who like to earn money and those that only wants to make it impossible for other people to do so. I prefer to have to deal with the first kind." Whether this statement is true, or not—I do not know.

However, it is possible that there were Jews or Jewish companies that for some reasons did not like Ivar Kreuger. I will give some indications to support this statement and several additional telegrams for support will be quoted further on.

April 29th 1931 Krister Littorin, CEO of STAB, sent the following cable to Mr. Durant of Lee Higginson & Co, New York.
    "432 we have a feeling that the rumors were spread by Singer & Friedlander, London and Lisser & Rosencrantz, Amsterdam both known as operators in baisse on a large scale in intimate cooperation stop in Stockholm they are working through Jacobson & Ponsbach, but also through Josephson & Co stop all these firms are Jewish and are told to have connections with Wertheim & Co in New York stop the unsure feeling to day in London and on the continent is supposed to partly depend on the report from us steel with regard to the first quarter and its pessimistic opinion about the immediate future stop the first opening finished 24 1/8 buyer and 3/16 seller turnover only 2875 which is satisfactory stop a decrease is however expected during the day. Littorin"

The Murder of Ivar Kreuger

The following is an excerpt from a letter by Mr. Thor Charlander, dated March 1st 1932 (sent from Paris to Mr. Dardel, Geneva and to Mr. Carl Frisk, Stockholm).

" . . . Apart from this I have nothing of interest to tell, with the exception that the day before yesterday I heard that a certain baisse party—Levy and others—once again have started their operations against the securities of the Kreuger Group. I suppose that this is the same Jewish consortium that works from Zurich, Switzerland.

The well known author, Anders Byttner, writes:

"Especially during the last phase of the drama the banker Olof Aschberg was running an absolutely fanatic scandal-mongering campaign against Ivar Kreuger and the Kreuger Group." Aschberg is said to be THE personal banker, who represented and supported the Bolshevik Regime, and handled their financial affairs out of Paris.

According to information received from a court trial in France, the banking firm of Steinfeld & Krumm was participant in the forgery of documents in connection with various securities in the Kreuger Group. They had collaborated with the banker Daniel Dreyfus and others. Dreyfus had in France replaced non marketable debentures with forged French certificates of deposit. These forged documents were sold to America where they were exchanged for American certificates of deposit. All transactions took place in a great hurry as it seemed that the American market, at that time, could not get enough of debentures—possibly for covering short sales.

Further on we will take a look at the acts of Mr. Joseph Sachs (Member of the Board of Stockholms Enskilda Bank).

I am quite sure that you could find several additional Jewish firms that were acting against the Kreuger Group and earned substantial amounts on short sales, traded with blocked collaterals and traded with forged certificates of deposit, etc. But I think that the Jewish firms were basically intermediaries following orders from powerful clients, who were acting to break up the Kreuger Group. I do not believe that they were acting on their own.

The Morgan Group is said to have tried to block all credits for Kreuger ever since Kreuger lent France $75 million at a considerably lower rate than that offered by Morgan. As mentioned above Morgan and his allies are said to be among those who gained the most from the crash of the Kreuger conglomerate. Wallenberg's' and their allies were getting in on a good second place, if one can believe the statistics. This, however, does not lessen the critics against the Jewish firms, but I fail to see a great conspiracy.

Ivar Kreuger and the Boliden mine

The Boliden project—as far as we know—was the last major Swedish project in which Ivar Kreuger was engaged. I, therefore feel, it is interesting to describe it a bit closer. Future research will quite possibly show that this project could have had an important connection to Ivar Kreuger's "removal" from the financial markets.

Quite a lot has been written about Boliden and Ivar Kreuger and a few have also written their doctoral thesis on the subject. These writings have one thing in common; they describe the Boliden transaction as complicated, mixed up and filled with mistakes. All these shortcomings have of course been blamed on Kreuger. Have the authors and candidates been right in what they have written? No, hardly. Unquestionably, mix ups and mistakes were made, but most of these were created after the death of Ivar Kreuger by investigators, administrators and lawyers. Apparently, they did not have the necessary knowledge, urge or simply did not care, to study the case sufficiently and to analyze all information available, before drawing their conclusions. Or—and this has happened before—they were simply told and paid for writing what was wanted of them.

Let us—in condensed form—take a look at some of the Boliden facts.

Boliden as a mining company

Skelleftea Gruv AB was formed on July 30, 1925 and was based on the operations of Centralgruppens Emissionsbolag that began in 1918. In 1926 there was an attempted merger with Vasterbottens Gruv AB, which however failed. In 1927 the name of Boliden was adopted and the share capital was increased to SEK 2,400,000 at a subscription rate of 120%. In 1928 the construction of a new smelting plant at Ronnskar began. Kreuger & Toll designed and built the large arsenic magazine and the docks. In the fall of 1929 Ivar Kreuger bought the majority of the shares in the mining companies. During 1930 the merger between the two mining companies was carried out (under the influence of Ivar Kreuger) and the name Bolidens Gruvaktiebolag was adopted. A new issue was made at nom. SEK 6,000,000 to 200% with payment before the end of 1931. On the 18th of June 1930 the first copper was delivered from the new smelter and on the 24th in the same month the works were in full production. In 1932 Boliden was practically a debt free company. In 1933 Boliden paid a dividend of SEK 5:—(1932 year's profit SEK 8,134,536.38)

Year	Net profit (SEK)	Bank	Cash	Dividends
1933	18,009,410	5,454,844	9,045	15%
1934	18,917,599	15,946,850	8,773	20%
1935	10,087,619	11,376,915	12,303	*
1936	8,117,665	10,934,392	20,485	15%
1937	16,610,003	14,663,526	4,994	15%
1938	9,325,325	23,677,986	7,602	15%
1939	22,769,951	28,880,168	4,256	15%
1940	23,521,193	27,184,240	10,118	15%
1941	22,025,780		2,424	15%
1942* * *	19,259,785	19,776,178:—**	2,892	12%
1943	15,587,380	5,534,301		12%
1944	15,989,663	6,108,160		12%
1945	15,306,494	22,885,839		12%
		29,513,296		

* In 1935 the share capital amounted to SEK 42,000,000 with reserve capital booked at SEK 39,600,000 and an amortization fund of SEK 9,400,000

Jonas Angstrom

** In 1941 Boliden invests some of its funds on the Swedish stock market—buying the shares listed below

* * *From 1942-1945 incoming dividends are booked at an average of SEK 550.000:—per year.

Nr of shares	Company name	Nr of shares	Company name
20,000	Granges/Oxelosund	2,500	Bofors
4,500	SKF	30,000	Reymersholm
5,000	Uddeholm	7,500	Volvo
3,500	Hoganas Billesholm	200	Skanska Cement
2,000	Stora Kopparberg	1,000	Sandviken
2,000	Stockholms Superfosf.	600	Stockholms Brygg.
2,000	ASEA	SEK nom. 6 million	Government. Bonds

Year by year the stock portfolio was increased.

As can be seen from the above figures, Boliden was a very sound company with a big potential that generated good profits and maintained a good dividend for its shareholders. When the profits some years were a bit lower, the company used ore with a somewhat lower mineral content in order to even out the ore reserve.

Any talk that Ivar Kreuger was unable to finance the operation of Boliden is, as you can see for yourself—pure nonsense. Boliden was financing itself.

Ivar Kreuger's acquisition of Boliden

In the coming section you will note that I quote several different persons giving roughly the same statements at one or several different occasions. There is a reason for this. After the death of Ivar Kreuger, the investigators and the administrators, and for that matter also some authors and doctoral candidates, claim that Ivar Kreuger did not personally buy Boliden. Pro and con arguments were continuing until the 12 of June 1936, when the matter was settled in court. The judgment was based on the fact that Ivar Kreuger's estate did not care to show that they had the better right to the shares, before a certain date. Rightly or wrongly—that is the way the judgment was made.

However, before the judgment was made the parties in question had come to an agreement. Why the procedures in court continued—I do not know—but possibly there were some additional legal fees that should be paid.

For several reasons, it is interesting to follow this case, as it is a good example of the principle that was adopted in the whole Kreuger affair, and that is: "Why make something simple, if there is a possibility to complicate it."

In the early parts of the 1920^s Kreuger began to purchase shares in the two mining companies, Vasterbottens Gruv Aktiebolag and Skelleftea Gruv Aktiebolag. His major acquisition was made during the second part of 1929, in a transaction with Skandbanken (Skandinaviska Kredit Aktiebolaget). Kreuger had a genuine interest in, what later became Boliden, and did not see it as an object for pure speculation—as some of his opponents have claimed. This fact is supported by the way he contacted and negotiated with some of the world's largest and most important mining companies prior to his final acquisition. The mineral deposits that were found in the Boliden area were of a complex ore type. In those years, there were only two major companies that could handle this type of ore in a commercial way. They were, Freiburg in Germany and American Smelting and Refining Corp., in Tacoma, USA (belonging to the Guggenheims'). Companies in England, France and Canada had shown interest in the development of new smelters. Boliden, however, realized the importance of being able to be independent and to be in full control of its own economy. For these reasons a new smelter was built at Ronnskar, which has developed into one of the best in the world.

Guggenheim's were specialists in this specific, complex, type of ore, which was the basis of Boliden Mining Co. They had at an early stage shown an interest in this new deposit. In a cable from September 26th 1929 where Kreuger describes the situation, the following can be read:

Extract:
" . . . . Our experts are now investigating Boliden and I hope to have full information available on my arrival in Stockholm stop It seems already now certain that the available ore justifies the present market price of the shares which is about seven hundred percent of par but there are possibilities that the ore supply will be at least ten times the proven supply which would make the proposition exceedingly interesting stop I had some time ago a visit in Stockholm by Capelin Smith of Guggenheim Brothers who proposed that I start with them a large American Holding Company based on the Boliden property stop His company American Smelting and Refinery Company has for some time been buying ore from Boliden and he has been secretly collecting information about the property stop Capelin Smith seems convinced that Boliden can be made into a very large proposition stop For different reasons we would not be willing to start such an American Holding Company at the present time but might consider such a plan after a few years stop Kreditbolaget has following assets which we have been negotiating to acquire first Boliden and other mining properties . . . ."

On the 1st of October Kreuger sends the following telegram to Capelin Smith, Claridge Hotel, in London
"Referring your letter September twenty-fifth I regret very much being unable to send you reports regarding Boliden at present stop As you may know Kreuger & Toll have for a long time been negotiating via Skandinaviska Kreditaktiebolaget regarding acquisition of the Boliden company and Kreditbolaget takes the position that the negotiations should be concluded before any new party is brought into the discussion stop While they therefore are willing to give us for our own information all reports available they do not like us to communicate these reports to other parties until we have decided that we want to acquire the mines stop As soon as this question has been settled one way or the other I will communicate with you again."

From a report to Kreuger, regarding Boliden, dated October 9th 1929, the following can be noted:
" . . . According to these (various reports) the body of ore is now well investigated down to 90 meters. From that level there is a blind shaft drilled to the 130 meter level. On this level it has been determined that the so called a-d-deposit, which consists of

the mines characteristic arsenic pyrites and which on account of its vastness is almost decisive for the value of the mine, covers an area of at least 600 sq. meters. The deposits on this floor are not yet fully utilized meaning that it could be anticipated that the area will contain the same amounts as those on levels above. At the depth of 50 meters, the area of the deposits is 675 sq. meters with gold content of 39.7 grams per ton and at the depth of 90 meters the area is 785 sq. meters with 65.3 grams gold per ton. The result from the 90 meter level must be even better considering the determined area, 600 sq. meters, and considering that the gold content has increased to 80 grams per ton. With the knowledge that the deposits go to the 130 meter level and with the knowledge of the ore body's regular form and character down to the 90 meter level, I believe that we can be fairly sure that the deposit will keep its area to a depth of 170 meter. It is of great importance to note that the content of gold has increased continuously . . .

G Magnusson"

About two year later Mr. Magnusson made the following rough estimate which proved to be quite close to the real conditions.

Sales value for 12,450 ton Cu 665	8,279,250
for 17,045 kg Au 2,400	40,908,000
for 40,080 kg Ag 35	1,402,800
for 150,000 ton sulphur pyrite 9	1,350,000
for 100,000 ton refined material	500,000
Total earnings (SEK)	52,440,050
Costs	31,188,000
Net profits for dividends etc.	21,252,050
= percentage of share capital 42,000,000	50.6 %
Present holdings of Boliden shares at nom.	
50:—783,272 of a total of 840,000 equal to	
94%. The shares having been bought at an average of	
100:—The value thus circa	
78,000,000	

Signed September 15th 1931—G. Magnusson

Of course a number of evaluations have been made of Boliden prior and after 1932. They differ between SEK 100 million and SEK 400 million. The evaluations made by Guggenheims should be considered to be the most important as they also considered the future potential and possibilities for development.

Kreuger knew what he was talking about when he described the potential of Boliden for laymen. He based his knowledge on his own experience from other mining operations and on long discussions with experts and on their reports as well. It is quite natural that he gave Riksbanken information of the future potential, rather than talking about the past, when he negotiated the use of the shares of Boliden as collateral for a loan in the size of SEK 40 million.

This has however, been criticized, by the doctoral candidates—who, by the way, were paid for their doctoral reports. One of the candidates (Bjorn Gäfvert) wrote, when describing Kreuger's, above mentioned loan from Riksbanken, in October 1931, that Kreuger should have told the bank. " . . . the future potential was bright and the actual value of Boliden was much larger, than the loan (40 million), for which the shares were placed as collateral. This information was to a large extent fake and cosmetics." (Ref. page 115) And " . . . Kreuger gave a misleading evaluation of the Boliden Corporation in connection with the negotiations in October." (Ref. page 262)

Mr. Gafvert's writings show that he does not have sufficient knowledge of the subject; neither does it seem that he has been interested in studying the material that is available. The 17th September 1931 I.K. sent a memorandum to the Governor of the Riksbank, Mr. Ivar Rooth, covering the Kreuger Groups financial situation. The memorandum contains various reservations together with explanations. Information is also given with regard to the gold production in Boliden and how they are calculated to increase over time. Information that was proven to be correct. A little later the memorandum is foolowed up by Bolidens annual balance and a correction of the reserve capitals size compared to the share capital. There is furthermore a letter with information of how STAB's accept credits are amortized. From these letters it can be seen that Kreuger keeps in constant touch with Riksbanken and in no way is giving misleading information about the financial situation. (1430-1435)

The sad thing is that his paper is tied to the Historical Institution at the University of Stockholm, which means that students are getting the wrong impression of the situation. Kreuger's opponents (heirs to the original opponents) are still well financed and fighting him on all fronts.

Let us now look at the actual acquisition, and how it was organized. Kreuger bought not only the mining shares from Skandinaviska Kreditaktiebolaget, but also many other stock holdings. The reason for this large acquisition is, as follows. During the period around the 1920s the banks through their subsidiaries had to take over large holdings in various Swedish industrial corporations. As time went by, these engagements became a heavy financial burden for the banks and showed up as not very attractive accounts on the balance sheets. Skandinaviska Kreditaktiebolaget turned therefore to

Ivar Kreuger and discussed with him the possibilities of his assistance in handling these investments. This case was similar to when Kreuger organized SCA (Swedish Cellulose Corp). He had bought various assets from Handelsbanken and merged them into one, large corporation with a big potential for the future.

The easiest way to describe this acquisition and possibly also the most correct way is to give an extract from the notes of Mr. Holger Lauritzen and the letters that were exchanged between Ivar Kreuger and Oscar Rydbeck (bank director of Skandbanken). It is impossible to get closer to the original source. At the same time, it would be impossible for Kreuger's opponents to claim something other than what actually was agreed between the parties. Not that it has prevented them from doing so. Now the readers can see for themselves how things were.

Lauritzen writes:
    "Some time in the beginning of 1929 there was quite a lot of talk about Boliden also in other countries. On one occasion there was a proposal from a source closely related to the Stockholm's Enskilda Bank (Wallenberg's) to act as an intermediary in a possible purchase of Boliden.

The summer of 1929, when I was abroad, Kreuger and Rydbeck discussed the possibilities for Kreuger to purchase Boliden. When the above mentioned inquiry came up, the question was taken up for reexamination together with a new discussion regarding the acquisition of the bank's other large stock holdings.

During the negotiations of the sale of Boliden, we asked Kreuger what his plans were for the Board of Directors and similar things. He declared that everything should remain as it was and that the shares also should remain registered on Hereditas (one of the bank's subsidiaries). This also tallied with Kreuger's wish to keep the transaction secret, until further notice. Director Magnusson should be permitted to be present at board meetings in order to be able to report to Kreuger.

—

"Kreuger had once said: "Sooner or later Kreuger & Toll will probably take over the shares". This was under no circumstances a condition for the transaction, but only a hint of his plans. Other possibilities, than to sell the shares to Kreuger & Toll, were not excluded. This was revealed by the fact that Kreuger during 1930 and 1931 was in touch with the Guggenheim Brothers in New York, whose engineers made long and far reaching research and investigations of the mine. I anticipated that a decision—one way or the other—would not be taken prior to the merger of the two mining companies."

—

"I can remember that at one, or possible several occasions during 1930, having asked Kreuger if it was the intention that Kreuger & Toll should take over the mining company during this year and received the answer that this was unlikely. "I do not know, but I do not think so," was Kreuger's reply.

—

"Later on during the year it became clear to me that a sale during the year was not going to take place. Partly on account of the rather time consuming investigations, that were taking place around the mine by Guggenheims engineers, and partly because the merger between the two mining companies was proceeding very slowly. Rightly or wrongly—I was of the opinion that the question of a sale to Kreuger & Toll was not of immediate interest until the merger had taken place."

(The merger was finalized on December 29th 1930. The combined mining company adopted the name of Bolidens Gruvaktiebolag).

—

The following statements were made in connection with the new issue of SEK 6,000,000 in Boliden.

"If the intention had been that Kreuger & Toll should own the shares, that were subscribed, it would have been more natural that the company had subscribed in its own name."

—

Kreuger & Toll handled the practical details in connection with the purchase of the shares in the two mining companies and in connection with the new issue—but for the account of Ivar Kreuger.

"To my knowledge, there were no negotiations, nor statements that could give the impression that Kreuger & Toll were acting for their own account, and not for the account of Ivar Kreuger."

" . . . I never thought it strange that Kreuger & Toll was the creditor for the shares in question, as I was of the opinion, that they had taken on the task, to handle all work in connection with the merger and the new issue, for the account of Ivar Kreuger, and that they were going to report everything to Kreuger in the end."

(HL)

Ivar Kreuger's first letter to Skandbanken, concerning the purchase of Boliden and other issues.

"October 31st 1929
IK/BK

Mr. Bank Director Oscar Rydbeck,
Stockholm

Brother,
    With reference to our previous negotiations regarding the possible take over from Skandinaviska Kreditaktiebolaget of certain blocks of shares, I herewith want to present the following suggestion:
    I, the undersigned, propose to acquire per December 15th 1929:

160,000 shares in Skelleftea Gruvaktiebolag with a par value of Kr 50:—per share, at a price of Kr 310:—each	49,600,000.-
40,000 shares in Vasterbottens Gruvaktiebolag with a par value of Kr 50:—per share, at a price of Kr 100:—each.	4,000,000.-
21,000 shares in Trafikaktiebolaget Grangesberg/Oxelosund at a price of Kr 360:—each	7,560,000.-
135,000 shares in AB Svenska Kullagerfabriken, Serie A at a price of Kr 250:—each	33,750,000.-

The payment for the above mentioned shares should be made with 20% on December 15th 1929 and with 20% on December 15th each of the years 1930, 1931, 1932 and 1933. On outstanding amount a 6% interest should be calculated payable every six months. These conditions of payments tally with the agreement made with AB Svenska Handelsbanken that recently was closed between this bank and AB Kreuger & Toll.

I take it for granted that at the purchase of the above mentioned assets, the undersigned, will also receive an option until December 31st 1931 to acquire all outstanding shares in Langrors Aktiebolag at a price of SEK 2,500,000:—and against a guarantee for Skandinaviska Kredit-Aktiebolaget's claims on the Marma-Langrors joint venture. This should be done in a, for the bank, satisfactory way. The option should also cover all outstanding shares in AB Zinkgruvor at a price of 150% of par.

It is assumed that all the assets of the Marma-Langrors joint venture, directly or indirectly, are owned by Langrors Aktiebolag, and that the sale of the products of the Marma-Langrors joint venture will be assigned to the Kreuger & Toll, newly organized Group for wood—and forest products, already from January 1st 1930. Furthermore, that the calculation of interest on the bank's claims on the Marma-Langrors joint venture and AB Zinkgruvor remains on the same bases as until now.

In this connection I want to mention that I have discussed the question of the future manager for Bergvik-Ala and the Langrors joint venture, and I do not see any objections to offering Mr. Gerhard Versteegh this position when the present manager resigns.

Yours Sincerely
Ivar Kreuger" (RA)

Bank director Oscar Rydbeck's reply.

SAKNDINAVISKA KREDITAKTIEBOLAGET
Executive Offices
Stockholm November 2nd 1929

Herr Ingenior Ivar Kreuger
Stockholm

Brother,
   In connection with your letter dated October 31st and to yesterday's and today's negotiations between you, Mannheimer and me I will herewith confirm that the following agreement has been made with regard to your purchase of the below listed stocks, that are in question, from Skandinaviska Kreditaktiebolaget or its subsidiary companies.

1)   *Skelleftea Gruv Aktiebolag and Vasterbottens Gruv Aktiebolag*
   We will take, as soon as possible, the necessary steps to merge these two companies. The merger should be made according to the following lines. Vasterbottens Gruv Aktiebolag offers Skelleftea Gruv Aktiebolag's share holders 7 shares in Vasterbottens Gruv Aktiebolag against two shares in Skelleftea Gruvaktiebolag or Kr 700:—cash. Vasterbottens Gruv Aktiebolag's share capital will thus amount to nom. 36,000,000. The name of the company could later on be changed either to Skelleftea Gruv Aktiebolag or any other suitable name. Already at this time you acquire from Skandinaviska Kreditaktiebolaget all shares in Skelleftea Gruv Aktiebolag and Vasterbottens Gruv Aktiebolag that it at present, directly or indirectly, owns. That is circa 152,000 shares in Skelleftea Gruv Aktiebolag and circa 38,000 shares in Vasterbottens Gruv Aktiebolag. The price for the shares being

for Skelleftea Gruv Aktiebolag SEK 350:—each, and for the shares of Vasterbotten Gruv Aktiebolag SEK 100:—each. These blocks contain all the A-shares in both companies. In the case that additional shares will be redeemed, you guarantee that you will acquire them at the same price.

2) 21,000 shares in *Trafikaktiebolaget Grangesberg-Oxelosund* at a price of SEK 360:—each, plus accrued interest according to earlier agreement for option. Furthermore, you receive an option to acquire prior to the end of 1931 the following blocks of shares:

3) circa 27,000 shares in *Stora Kopparberg's Bergslags Aktiebolag* at a price of SEK 250.—each, plus accrued interest of 6% from the 15th of December 1929 until the day that the option is called, with the deduction of dividends received during the time.

4) circa 135,000 shares in *Aktiebolaget Svenska Kullagerfabriken* at a price of SEK 250:—each, plus accrued interest of 6% from the 15th of December 1929 until the day the shares are paid with deduction of dividends received during the time. Regarding these shares you should be obliged to—if we so ask—pick them up at a price of Kr 240.—each plus accrued interest of 6% from the 15th of December 1929, but with deduction of dividends received during the time.

5) The shares in Langrors Aktiebolag that, directly or indirectly, belong to the bank, consists of 1,000 pref. shares and 555 common shares, each with a face value of SEK 1,000, to a price of SEK 3,500,000 plus accrued interest of 6% from the 15th of December 1929, until the day, when the option is called, with deduction of dividends received during the time. At the time these shares are acquired you are also obliged to secure the Marma joint venture's debts in a suitable manner. During the time of the option the bank guarantees not to change the present conditions for the running interest on the credit. The interest is at present 6% and will during the time of the option be 1/2% above the rate of Riksbanken's[8] three month rate of discount.

6) The total share capital of Aktiebolaget Zinkgruvor—4,000 pc. with a face value of SEK 1,000—, at a total price of SEK 5,000,000 plus 6% interest from the 15th of December 1929 until the day the option is called with deduction of possibly received dividends. In connection with this the bank has informed you that Aktiebolaget Zinkgruvor, apart from their own debts also is responsible for Trollhattans Electrothermiska Aktiebolag's total debts. The bank guarantees not to charge Aktiebolaget Zinkgruvor's and Trollhattans Electrothermiska Aktiebolag a higher rate of interest on their debts, than 1/2% above the discount rate charged by Riksbanken, at any time during the period that the option is valid.

The bank does not have any number of shares worth mentioning of Telefonaktiebolaget L M Ericsson.

---

[8]   Swedish Federal Reserve Bank

The payment of your firm purchase of shares should be made with 40% cash on December 15th 1929. For the remaining part you will have 5 years of credit at a rate of interest that will be 1% higher than the discount rate of Riksbanken, at any time during this period. For this credit you should furthermore be obliged to arrange with the guarantee by Kreuger & Toll from the beginning of next year. The shares should remain in the custody of the bank as security for the credit. When one or several of the above mentioned options are called, the payment should be made in the same manner.

Regarding the management of Skelleftea Gruv Aktiebolag and Vasterbottens Gruv Aktiebolag you have expressed that you at the present time do not want any changes. With the exception, that Director Magnusson at the next ordinary board meeting ought to be elected a member of the Board. You have received information that the salaries, currently paid to Director Falkman, Doctor Lindblad, Director Wesslau, Doctor Backstrom and Chief engineer Palén, are temporary and at a low level, and should be adjusted as soon as the company is in full operation, which probably will be from the beginning of next year.

With regard to the Marma Joint Venture, you have informed me that your intentions are that after a planned merger between this Joint Venture and the Bergvik Ala Nya Aktiebolag has been completed, Director Gerard Versteegh should be given the management.

This letter is only intended to be a confirmation of the broad lines of the agreement made and will, as soon as it is approved by my Board, be followed by a detailed contract. I enclose a copy of this letter, which I would be grateful to get in return with your signature as an agreement.

Yours Sincerely,
O Rydbeck"
(BA)

Below are some additional extracts that are of a certain importance:

"In September 1931 Ivar Kreuger was asked by Skandinaviska Kredit AB if it was the intention that Kreuger & Toll should take over Boliden during the year. If that were the case—a change of what had happened would not be necessary. IK replied that it might be possible, but that nothing had been decided. No further discussion was made in this case and things were organized in connection with the rearrangements of credit in September."

(HL)

From a court record:
"After the evidence given by Mr. Abenius (lawyer) and Mr. Lindhagen (Supreme Court Justice) the court was informed that Ivar Kreuger had intended to keep a part of his shareholdings in Boliden."

(Extract from RR October 10th 1933).

"Mr. Durant (Lee Higginson) gave evidence that Ivar Kreuger during the spring of 1930 had told Durant that he had acquired the majority in his own name. Kreuger & Toll, however, had an option to buy his interests."

"The reason for Kreuger's visit to New York in December 1931 was, according to Durant, to discuss a plan through which Kreuger & Toll could acquire Boliden in exchange for participating debentures."

"The shares of Boliden are, as you know owned by me personally, but Kreuger & Toll has an option to acquire them from me."
(Telegram to Durant, Lee Higginson) November 14th 1931).

Extract from an enclosure made by the lawyer Forssner to the court of appeal in October 1935, page 77.

"As shown, Ivar Kreuger owned between 93 and 94% of the total share capital of Boliden. It has never been claimed that he sold his complete holding or a certain quota thereof. Only that he sold 80% or circa 80% of the total amount of shares of Boliden, that is 672,000 shares or approximately this number."

The other doctoral candidate, Jan Glete wrote:" He never had any thought of making the acquisition for his own account outside the ordinary business of the Group", (*How could possibly Glete know anything about this?*). A little further on Glete continues:" In this case one will have to be satisfied with the legal situation and note that the courts in two instances have judged that the shares belonged to Kreuger & Toll. Possibly Kreuger did not see it that way, but it was his own fault that there had been a mix up."

I find it difficult to follow Jan Glete's reasoning, as it lacks in logic. (Jan Glete has written a whole book about Boliden and is considered an authority on the subject. However, apparently he did not avail himself of all existing material. (Alternatively, certain sources have expressed a wish that he should divert (emphasize the illegality) somewhat from the truth, in order not to disturb their interests).

Why do I spend so much time on the above details? Various authors—the people that have been paid to know—have described Ivar Kreuger as a business man, who only looked for big fat profits. He used to rush into a company that he had bought, fire the management and plunder the company of its assets. He lied and deceived banks, company managers, financiers, presidents, politicians, accountants and whomever you can think of. He was ruling a joint venture of more than 160 companies, all over the world, and he forged most of the balance sheets. He was never given a chance to defend himself against the more serious charges that were manufactured after his death.

If you stop to think for just one minute you will find that according to Ivar Kreuger's opponents, he spent a lot of time on worthless matters. They seem to have forgotten the time he spent on building up the Swedish (and other) industries, forming interesting mergers, etc. thereby creating monopolies and providing big loans to entire countries. In accordance with his opponents, the World seemed to have been filled with incompetent and ignorant people (on all levels) during the first thirty years of the nineteen hundreds.

My intention with my writings is through research to assemble facts; small as well as large, put them together and hopefully find the truth. The truth of how Kreuger was as a person, the truth about his business as well as the material presented by his opponents, the way they worked and their businesses.

According to my research, we are getting a completely different picture of the financial history than what some people have previously wanted us to believe.

During the fall of 1931 something strange happened in the Boliden affair. Could it possibly be something due to a non-recurring circumstance—or? It is just as well, that I allow bank director Lauritzen, through his notes, to describe what happened:

"Some time, either before my departure June 15th or immediately after my return September 1st 1931, I had a talk with Kreuger with regard to the securities held for him and his companies' business with the bank. The question of the Boliden shares came up and Kreuger mentioned that he to his surprise had found that his promissory note for which the shares in Boliden were used as collateral had at some time been changed against a promissory note issued by Kreuger & Toll. This, he said, had been done without his knowledge and he had just recently been informed about it. I was very surprised and promised to find out what had happened. After a talk with Brunell it was confirmed that an exchange had taken place after a discussion between him and director Sjostrom at Kreuger & Toll, in January of the same year. The exchange of the notes, were apparently caused by a misunderstanding, and I informed Kreuger that a correction should be made as soon as possible. In connection with this question I asked him if it was the intention that Kreuger & Toll should take over Boliden during the year in which case it would not be necessary to change the notes again. Kreuger replied that it could be possible but that nothing was decided in this matter. There was no further discussion in this particular matter."

You could of course describe this as an example of confusion and wrong doings, or whatever—but it would be hard to blame this on Ivar Kreuger.

Let me once again quote what the doctoral candidates have written and compare it with what actually took place.

In his paper, Bjorn Gäfvert, maintains that Ivar Kreuger at several occasions had given wrong information, among others, to Riksbanken, with regard to the Group's economical situation. Therefore he had been forced to return with renewed requests for larger loans, than those he had said that he needed from the beginning. Gäfvert also stated that Kreuger was aware of a weak period in the liquidity during the months of February and March 1932.

I will again quote Lauritzen when he describes a meeting at Riksbanken, at which he was present. Kreuger had been asked to attend in order to answer some questions.

"During the meeting several questions were directed to Kreuger, who answered all in his usual businesslike manner.

—

"Thereafter Kreuger was asked if he believed that the Group would be in need of additional large credits. On this question he had difficulties to give a firm reply. His Group had borrowed large amounts of money, very large sums had already been repaid, but everything was very closely dependent on the development of the market in America, which at the present time was more or less closed down. "I hope that it will be enough with what we have received but I can of course not guarantee anything."

Kreuger's negotiations with Riksbanken resulted in a loan of SEK 40 million, according to the following agreement. The shares of Boliden were placed as collateral.

"As security for a maximum credit of 40 million against drafts issued by me and accepted by STAB and AB Kreuger & Toll, which credit was granted me by Riksbanken according to the decision of the Board of Governors of Riksbanken on October 24th I herewith pledge as security 84,000 A-shares, SEK 4,200,000 and 735,513 B-shares, SEK 35,175,650 in Boliden together with coupons. I consent that if any of the drafts in question should not be paid at maturity Riksbanken should be able to, without hearing me and without the observance of the formalities stated by law, sell the securities at auction or at a

Securities Exchange and from the proceeds repay the capital and interest as well as costs for the handling and sale of the securities.

Stockholm October 24th 1931
Ivar Kreuger
Witnessed:
K Bokman, Krister Littorin"

There is an obvious difference between what actually happened and what Gäfvert insinuated.

The Reorganization of Credits

Some time after the meeting at Riksbanken Kreuger and Lauritzen discussed the possibilities, to change the collateral, for the credits that the bank had allowed, and replace them with securities that were independent in nature from the Group.

Lauritzen writes in his notes that he presented the following suggestion: " . . . Even if foreign bonds of a large amount were to be offered us for this purpose, I am willing to accept them, preferably such bonds that you have received against the credits that we have been giving."

Kreuger promised to present a suggestion for the change and a strengthening of the collateral accordingly.

Lauritzen continues: "One or two days later, possibly September 10th, Kreuger called and wanted a meeting with regard to the credits. I suggested that I should look him up at STABs office . . . Kreuger began the discussion with approximately the following words: 'You expressed a wish that I should exchange all the shares in companies belonging to the Group against other securities. I would, however like to get out all Swedish shares that are deposited in your bank as collateral and if I have understood you correctly, you would not have anything against accepting German Government Bonds in their place. What do you say about this suggestion?'
  I replied: "Do you mean the shares in Grängesberg and SKF?"—
— "Yes, and also the shares in Boliden, if that is possible."—
— "No. I am afraid that we could not submit the shares in Boliden. Furthermore, I do not understand how this transaction could be possible, as it under all circumstances will be a matter of rather large sums."
— "Well, I will tell you, as it is. I have been talking to Littorin and Bergman, who together with me are on the Board of International Match Corporation (IMCO)*, and we have decided to use $50 million of German Bonds that now are in the portfolio of IMCO. At present they can hardly be used as collateral for a loan in America, so they could better be used here."

---

* Ivar Kreuger was President, Littorin and Bergman Vice-Presidents all three were Directors.

47

'I did, of course, not think that the issue was anything but an exchange of securities between IMCO and the other companies within the Group. However, the amount seemed very large to me.'

— "It is quite clear that the security that you are talking about should be sufficient to cover very substantial sums, but I hardly believe that we could accept such a large amount of German Bonds as security for the loans."

Kreuger smiled and said that he did not intend to offer the whole block as collateral for the credits in the bank. "We have a lot of other securities to offer as well, but perhaps you will be kind enough to think it over and let me know what quantity of German Bonds you will accept in this case."

In this connection, Kreuger gave specific information regarding what portions of the lump sum credit that was going to fall on the different members of the Group, i.e. STAB, Kreuger & Toll, and Kreuger himself. In previous credit grants, especially in connection with the $35 million credit, all drafts had been issued by Kreuger and accepted with 50% by STAB and 50% by Kreuger & Toll. When the whole question of credit now was reorganized, it was quite natural that a separation between the creditors was made at the same time, in relation to the amounts they had received from the credit. This meant a substantial reduction of the credits of Kreuger & Toll and a substantial increase of the credits of STAB and Ivar Kreuger, used in connection with the options for SKF, the new issue in Boliden etc.

In all discussions with Riksbanken, as well as in connection with the Polish credit, it was assumed that, the debtor's name was going to be held at disposal in proportion to what was considered suitable in connection with the credit.

All credits were now going to be split, so that one company did not provide a guarantee for the other, as had previous been the case. All current engagements were herewith brought into compliance. In my opinion this was not only a change of the bank's collateral, but also a clearing between the companies, and between the companies and Kreuger. This must be seen as an extraordinarily natural act for anybody that had been present and observed the summary procedure in connection with the original credit of the $35 million as it was split 50/50 between STAB and Kreuger & Toll. Now however the credits were divided between the three parties, the companies and Kreuger, himself, in accordance with a specification made by Kreuger.

We agreed, that I should make a specification over which amounts of suggested collateral the bank thought necessary in order to accept the proposed suggestion, regarding the release of securities, the reorganization of engagements and for the cover of the payments of SKF and the new issue in Boliden. The real estate company Hufvudstaden, the common shares of IMCO and a block of the Rumanian Institute of Monopolies bonds were also under consideration. Kreuger expressed a wish that a block of the Young bonds to the value of SEK 10 million that the bank held, should be returned. That meant that a block of German Bonds to the value of $40 million should be pledged. The 14th of September this matter was discussed at a lunch meeting at the bank between Kreuger and me. He suggested that the amount of German Bonds should be reduced to $30 million which I accepted when certain other securities—Rumanian Bonds, I believe—had been added.

With regard to the Boliden shares I can not say that they were discussed in connection with the credit reorganization. It was completely clear, that they should be returned to Kreuger as correction of the change, which had taken place in the month of January, and in this connection, his personal debts increased, and Kreuger and Tolls debts decreased with the corresponding amount.

The Bank inspectors expressed to me their satisfaction with the way the credits had been reorganized, and his assumption that the Riksbanken's fears for the credits, as far as the risks were concerned, would disappear. I probably informed the Governor of Riksbanken as well about the situation."

As Kreuger was going abroad he delegated to director Erik Sjostrom (K&T) to arrange the details in connection with the exchange of collateral:
"To Skandinaviska Kredit AB
Exchange of Collateral
For one thing: A block with face value $12,000,000 of German Reich 6% External Loan of 1930, for my account, in the name of Skandinaviska Kredit AB deposited with Den Danske Landsmansbank Hypotek og Vekselbank, Copenhagen.

For another thing: The excess collateral in Boliden
October 26th 1931
Ivar Kreuger through E Sjostrom"

"For one thing: £1000,000 British Match Corp. for my account in the name of Skandinaviska Kredit AB's name deposited with Den Norske Creditbank, Oslo.
Ivar Kreuger through E Sjostrom"

This part, of the credit reorganization, which only concerns Boliden to a minor degree, is rather important. Kreuger's opponents and various authors have for years accused him—in fact they have even used words as "stolen" and "fraud"—in connection with the transfer of the German Bonds from IMCO's account to be used as collateral in

Skandbanken. It has also been said that this was done in secrecy and that nobody else than he himself was aware of this transfer. Therefore, I have thought it important to disclose what actually happened and that Kreuger accounted for his action to several people. When reading this section you should keep in mind that Kreuger had pledged his own private fortune as well in getting the credits for the companies of the Group. STAB's credits were to a certain extent supporting the assets of IMCO and STAB owned a major part of IMCO. Kreuger & Toll owned a major part of STAB and was in turn owned by Ivar Kreuger. From Kreuger's point of view the Group was in many cases treated as one unit each "component" supporting the others with collateral and/or funds when necessary.

Of course, the transfer as such was wrong, if you look upon it with the eyes of an accountant and also from a legal point of view—unless—and this is a big unless—there were documents supporting the action. Documents do have a tendency to sometimes disappear, if it is to the advantage of a case. I do not say that there have been such documents. They might have existed on a "tomorrow" basis. However, I would not be surprised if, in the future, I happened to find—at least a hint of them—during my research. Such is the condition of the main archive that even the most unexpected material can turn up in likewise unexpected places. I am not trying to defend the legal actions taken—as we do not know enough about them—but I want to have the situation as fully explained as possible and demonstrate that the move was quite logical.

It is also important to keep in mind that the reorganization of the credits with the bank was just a reorganization, and not a question of any new loans. It was an exchange of collateral. The Swedish securities, having been used as collateral for the Group's credits, were released and replaced with German Bonds that for the time being could not be pledged elsewhere, i.e. in the United States. If IMCO should still be the owners of the German Bonds or, if it was thought that these should be replaced with the Swedish securities that were released such as SKF, Grängesberg, STAB etc. we do not know today. It would have been a logical move. It is also possible that Kreuger in connection with his trip abroad gave the necessary instructions to Erik Sjostrom to handle this matter. Unfortunately there are several examples of similar situations where Sjostrom simply forgot what he was supposed to do. Another possibility is that Kreuger was going to give a special declaration of the case in connection with the bookkeeping at year's end. Any way, the important thing is that I have been able to prove that Ivar Kreuger did not make a secret of the transfer of the German Bonds. He talked to the members of the Board of IMCO, explained the situation to the bank, as the reorganization of the credits was a matter for the whole Group one way or the other and IMCO was a part of the Group.

In order to prove my point with regard to Erik Sjostrom, when saying that he not always did what he was supposed to do and when trying to correct often caused rather big distractions, I will allow myself to go one step ahead of events. The event I am going to describe, I have named "The mystery of the disappeared block of stocks", and this is what happened:

After the death of Ivar Kreuger the various groups of "investigators" immediately began to take an inventory of the contents in the vaults that were kept in the Group's different premises. These inventories were to a very large extent handled by the opponents of Ivar Kreuger and they were very careful in not signing any of the records even if there was a list over the people that were present. During my research I found a note that really puzzled me:

"In the room of the vault, Aktienbau Verein Nom. German Mark 6,000,000 Boliden Gruv AB 114,254 pc each SEK 50:-, 2,730 pc each SEK 1,000."

How could this be possible? All the shares in Boliden should according to all information have been placed as collateral in Riksbanken. On the other hand—is it possible to take an inventory and count items, which do not exist? This block was not mentioned in any of the bankruptcy documents. The inventory taken was a remarkable thing in it itself. Three people were separately going through the different boxes and they managed to find different items and quantities—in the same box—every so often. But the block of Boliden shares was such a large and important matter that it ought to have been noted in other places. Only one inventory list mentioned this block, but again it seemed impossible to me, that someone can count about 117,000 shares out of thin air.

I asked around. I consulted people that should know. Nobody could explain this mystery.

I have now found the explanation. Not where it should have been, but in a completely different connection. The explanation is as follows:

At the new issue in Boliden, the shares were delivered to Kreuger & Toll in order for the people that had subscribed to the shares to sign them in blank. Sjostrom was responsible for sending the shares to Riksbanken after the signing. However, he forgot all about it. Apparently the memory was bad in many places, as Riksbanken forgot to remind Kreuger & Toll about the shares. When the question of inventory came up and in fact was carried out March 15th 1932 Sjostrom quickly jumped into action and arranged with delivery to Riksbanken on March 18th. This explains why the shares were noted March 15th but not later. But it was not only the delivery to Riksbanken that Sjostrom forgot. He forgot to tell anybody about it. At that time Kreuger & Toll had received a moratorium and was under the control of the Government and apart from that there were the "investigators". None of these were informed. To authenticate this story, please see below.

"Receipt from Sveriges Riksbank
Stockholm March 18th 1932
To Kreuger & Toll
Vastra Tradgardsgatan 17, Stockholm

We have today received 39 boxes according to information containing 114,217 shares in Boliden Gruv AB and separately 37 shares in the same company. After examination of the boxes' contents, a special acknowledgement of having received the above mentioned stocks will be given."
Sveriges Riksbank
Unreadable signatures

(RA)

The way that Sjostrom handled this rather simple question led to a number of complications and the lawyers succeeded in getting it mixed into the question that was brought up in court about "better right". The fight was between Ivar Kreuger's and Kreuger & Toll's estates.

"In an address at the time of the trial June 4th 1935, page 115 the opposition has stated that the shares of the new issue of Boliden were transported to Riksbanken on March 18th 1932, with the permission of the Government controller, and therefore came to the conclusion that the shares belonged to Ivar Kreuger. Ernst Lyberg (Government controller) knew nothing of this (which had taken place without his knowledge) neither had the administrators given their permission."

(RA)

It should however be observed that all the shares were not accounted for.

Ivar Kreuger's sale of Boliden to Kreuger & Toll

In the late fall of 1931 Kreuger's plans for Boliden and its place in the Group had taken form and he decided to sell the major part of his holding to Kreuger & Toll and to accept payment in the form of participating debentures. The transaction was made in the form of a memorandum to the Board as per below:

"Minutes of the meeting November 19th 1931 with the Board of Directors of Kreuger & Toll

Present:

Ivar Kreuger, C. Juhlin-Danfelt, Ernst Kreuger, Paul Toll, O. Rydbeck, Krister Littorin, C. W. Andrén, Erik Sjöström and Nils Ahlström (titles omitted).

§ 1

As the annual general meeting previously had empowered the Board to issue participating debentures up to a total sum of 250,000,000 Swedish Crowns, the Board decided, based on this empowerment, that debentures of the same type as those that already had been issued, nominal value SEK 139,000,000, should be issued in an amount of nom. 80,833,340, through by which the total amount of issued debentures would amount to nom. SEK. 220.000,000.

§ 2

The Board decided that the mentioned amount of debentures nom. SEK 80,833.340:—at a suitable time should be listed on the exchanges of Stockholm, Amsterdam, Basel, Bern, Zurich, Lausanne, Geneva and London.

§ 3

In order to acquire 80% of the stocks of Bolidens Gruv Aktiebolag, the Board decided that the mentioned debentures nom. SEK 80,833,340:—should be issued at par to N.V.Financieele Matschappij Kreuger & Toll. The Board empowered thereafter Ivar Kreuger, Nils Ahlström and Erik Sjostrom to further decide how to proceed with the above mentioned decisions of the Board and to decide in other related questions.

§ 4

It was noted that Ivar Kreuger was not taking part of the Board's decision stated in §3. The minutes were immediately reviewed for accuracy, confirmed and signed.

(RA)

It is worth observing that Ivar Kreuger did not take part in the decision mentioned in §3. It should also be observed that there is nothing mentioned about the relationship between A—and B-shares, only that 80% of the shares of Boliden were acquired. Kreuger owned approximately 94%. It is decided that the debentures should be issued at par to N.V Financieele Matschappij Kreuger & Toll. There is however no mentioned of the rate at which the debentures should be sold to Kreuger. I do not think that you could expect him to pay more for the debentures than he paid for the shares of Boliden. There was no reason for him to donate funds to Kreuger & Toll. It can also be worth noting that this special issue of debentures was named "The Boliden issue".

Immediately after the above mentioned Board meeting Kreuger & Toll began to deliver debentures to banks, private bankers, brokers and other financial institutions. It has been stated that verbal orders were given by Ivar Kreuger for delivery of the debentures. Although Kreuger was abroad telegraphic instructions have been located and verified. A large part of these debentures were used to increase and change the collateral for loans where the previously given collateral had decreased in value due to the collapse of the stock market. Other parts were pledged for loans, and again other parts were placed with American companies in order to establish trading accounts. These accounts were going to begin trading when Kreuger & Toll made an official announcement with regard to its acquisition of Boliden and in connection with the Boliden issue of debentures.

The pledging and increasing of collateral with these debentures was a smart move by Kreuger. He stipulated that the debentures were not to be sold on the open market, but should be returned number for number the day he wanted to pay the debts. And there was also a small catch attached to these conditions. They could not be freely sold on any market. A certain form of registry was necessary. The effect of this was very negative for those that were engaged in short selling. They were caught in a corner and could not get out without help. Some of them even tried forgery. Some time before his death Ivar Kreuger had started legal actions against a French group of his opponents. They were put on trial and some of them were later sentenced to extended jail terms. But that is another story.

In connection with the Boliden issue of debentures we come in touch with another story that can be of great interest because it appears in many versions and I am quite sure it is giving us a lead. The question is whereto? The reason why I am going to let this story be a part of the Boliden affair is that Ivar Kreuger accepted a block of SEK16,000,000 in debentures, which previously had been put to his disposal by the Board, as part of the payment for the Boliden shares.

During the spring 1931 the Board of Kreuger & Toll had given Kreuger a sum of SEK 16,000,000 of debentures for his disposal in order to strengthen collateral and to put them on the market. It will take too long a time to explain the rather complex situation so you will for the moment have to be satisfied with this information. (*You will find a more detailed explanation in my earlier book*). During the summer Kreuger asked Sune Schéle—previously in charge of the market in India for the account of STAB—to be prepared to receive a block of debentures and to distribute or sell them on the European market. When Schéle received the debentures from the chief of the Investment Department, Mr. G Bergenstråhle, he signed a receipt that was actually intended for Erik Sjostrom in his capacity of Board member. Sjostrom had also been present at the Board meeting when it was decided that the block of debentures in question should be put to Kreuger's disposal. The explanation for the receipt and its content is somewhat unclear. It reads as follows:

"Receipt

I herewith confirm that I have received from director Erik Sjostrom various parcels said to contain, nom. SEK Sixteen million (16,000,000) Participating Debentures.

28,000/500	14,000,000
13,500/100	1,350,000
5,000/40	200,000
22,500/20	450,000
69,000	16,000,000

Signed, Stockholm July 10th 1931
Sune Schéle

Mr. Bergenstråhle at the Investment Department asked for two receipts from Erik Sjostrom. One that tallies with the one shown above and another one that only Bergenstråhle knew the text of. Of course the Investment Department kept an account book or journal. I have studied this journal and it does not tally with the reality neither to the numbers, nor to the nominal value of the debentures. Bergenstråhle noted the following in the ledgers for:

July 8th 1931
Delivered to dir. Sjostrom Nr 84,501-88,500 4,000 at 500:—= 2,000,000 and for:

Jonas Angstrom

July 10th 1931
Delivered to dir Sjostrom Nr 88,501-116,500 28,000 at 500:—= 14,000,000

(RA)

As you can see from these notes the original receipt and those noted in the ledgers do not agree. Nobody asked Bergenstråhle,—or for that matter Schéle—why. It might have been a little too sensitive. Especially, as Bergenstråhle might have been a sort of double agent.

Schéle's declaration regarding the disposal of the total 16,000,000 of debentures requires further research. However, without difficulties you can see that what he claims does not agree with the facts. At this moment we have to be satisfied with the information given by Schéle that he delivered approx. 5 million to Geoffrey Weinstein & Co, in Paris and exchanged 5 million in Koopmansbank, Amsterdam against other debentures with English stamps that previously had been deposited with the bank. Furthermore he claims to have sold 6,000,000 at a rate of 400% above par and accounted for about 13 million to Kreuger.

(PA)

Schéle's story changes from time to time. However, nobody has questioned it.— Until . . . . On December 23rd 1931 Kreuger had been informed of series of debentures on the market in NY that actually should not be there. He cabled to Stockholm in order to get additional information about these specific debentures.

"have got from bugge the numbers of the debentures deposited for white weld stop all debentures are for 500 crowns cash and numbers 106501 to 106900 107501 to 107900 108501 to 108680 108585 to 109975 11001 to 11165 110171 to 110970 111201 to 111400 111701 to 111900 113001 to 113800 114201 to 114403 stop please try if you can identify any of—".

(0571)

The same day he got the following reply:
"with the exception of 11001 to 11165 all the mentioned debentures come from the 16 million block but there is not a single one among those that I received stop possibly Sune can tell. Littorin".
(0572)

With a follow up from Durant to Krister Littorin
" . . . stop Ivar has discovered identity syndicate which sold so much stock short paris and believes is in position force covering—Dondurant".

You do not have to be Sherlock Holmes to realize that something fishy was going on behind Ivar Kreuger´s back. I will return to this matter a little later on.

In the Magistrates' Court, as well as in the Court of Appeal, this block of 16,000,000 in debentures has been questioned to a certain extent, without anybody getting more knowledgeable or happier. The following is quoted from a court record:

"Schéle left them (the debentures) for safe keeping in a special deposit box on the premises of STAB. The key to the deposit box was kept by STAB's treasurer. Some time after Schéle returned to Paris, Kreuger wished to dispose of the debentures in question wherefore the key, after the admittance of Schéle, was turned over to Kreuger. Kreuger had disposed of the total block of debentures and as far as available documents show nothing of this has been accounted for to Kreuger & Toll. At the time when the debentures were issued the going rate was 420%."

Another statement about the same block:
"A major part of these debentures have been used for the strengthening of collateral and there has hardly been any selling on the market."

Still another statement:
"These debentures have to a certain extent been sold but no larger amounts have been received until 1932. The issue should be used to acquire 80% of Boliden."

(RA)

As is evident from the court documents nothing agrees with the original information given by Schéle. Needless to say, none of these statements tally with the police records describing the questioning of Schéle. The case gets more complicated from lawyer to lawyer and from court to court. However, this is good example of how debts could be created and Kreuger be given the blame. This also shows how assets in the form of debentures disappeared, and why the Investment Department should have come in focus and been forced to account for what was missing. But the world did not want to see those problems. It saw only a newly made swindler, given the name of Ivar Kreuger. I can accept that we have to do with all sorts of swindlers but the name is completely wrong. The correct names will be found among his opponents.

Ivar Kreuger in New York

Kreuger went to the US in December 1931 in order to discuss an introduction of Boliden and the Boliden issue of debentures on the American market, through which Kreuger & Toll's acquisition of Boliden could be paid by means of debentures. Through such a transaction Kreuger would become liquid, by getting back some of the funds already invested. Kreuger's intentions are confirmed by Mr. Durant's statement (of Lee Higginson).

"The purpose of Kreuger's visit to New York in December was to discuss a plan through which Kreuger & Toll should be able to acquire the shares of Boliden against participating debentures."

(RA)

If, Kreuger were to succeed with his plans, the liquidity problems for the Group would be solved for the near future, and the transaction with Boliden should also strengthen the name and the position of Kreuger & Toll. This would also prepare the ground for additional interesting projects together with the Guggenheim's, Rockefeller's, Rothschild's and others. At the same time it would mean a serious blow to Kreuger's opponents and nothing less than a catastrophe for those that had been speculating against him. Kreuger would be in the position to repay certain loans, and demand to get the collateral in return—number for number.

1932

On January 1st 1932, Erik Sjostrom informed Ivar Kreuger that SEB (Stockholms Enskilda Bank/Wallenberg) had called and showed great interest in what Kreuger was doing with Boliden in New York.

On January 11th Marcus Wallenberg (there is no information available, if it was senior or junior) visited Kreuger & Toll in order to get additional information.

(RA)

On January 15, Ivar Kreuger got the following telegram from Paris:
"Kreugivar—New York USA Jan. 15th 1932 Ivar Kreuger Park Ave. Mrs. Hanaus Paper Forces* insinuates that information concerning Boliden are intended to give

58

public false impression that Boliden belongs to you full stop American correspondents here wish interview Ehrensvard on Boliden stop Bergius thinks Ehrensvard willing give statement if I write it for him stop—kindly telegraph—Cedershiold"

- This newspaper's business idea was to—against a satisfactory payment—spread negative rumors about almost anything.

The spreading of rumors and counteracting was increasing over the whole line. This issue had been noted over a long period of time*, but now the pressure had increased. However, there are no definite connections between the "fishing" for information in Stockholm, and the articles in the papers in Paris.

- "During 1931 the German Treasury Department turned to Marcus Wallenberg, Sr. for advice regarding actions to be taking in order to strengthen the economical situation in Germany. He advised, believe it or not, that Germany as a first measure should stop the interest payments of the Kreuger Group's loans to Germany."

(TK)

Ivar Kreuger continued his work in New York according to plans and was constantly in touch with leading and important people in Sweden reporting about the actual situation day by day. Parallel to the negotiations regarding Boliden, Kreuger discussed the possibilities for discounting the acceptance credits for SCA's account. In other words discussing the financing of SCA's and other Swedish forest industries export.

New York 1/15 1932 15.34 com
Governor of the Riksbank Ivar Roth, Karlavagen 48, Stockholm
"Thanks for the telegram stop regarding the cellulose credits I am working according to the lines you have given stop I have at present certain negotiations with regard to Boliden that look very promising but it is unknown how quickly they can mature stop the market feeling here has improved very much the last few days but you would probably have to wait one or two weeks before you can discuss foreign acceptance credits.
Kreugivar"

(PA)

New York 1/17 1932 nil wu
-Nlt—Minister of finance Felix Hamrin, Norrtullsgatan 3, Stockholm
On account of negotiations partly with regard to Boliden and partly with regard to the Cellulose company I have been delayed in America longer than I thought stop confidentially I can inform with regard to Boliden that the negotiations are aimed at selling 42,000 B-shares in Boliden to a large American industrial corporation with

important mining interests stop it is still too early to judge if this transaction can be fulfilled but the prospects are for the moment good stop a sale of this type should not . . . .
Kreuger

(PA)

New York 1/24 1932 nil com
-Nlt Sten Handelsbanken Stockholm
   Would like you to publish the article on Boliden and suggest that Magnusson should supply the necessary information stop we will during the next few days publish Kreutolls official take over of Boliden against the issue of nominal eighty million crowns of participating debentures stop the possibilities to be able to sell considerable amounts of these at satisfactory prices during the next three months seem rather good provided that the improving conditions of the market will remain in spite of the last days decline stop the negotiations regarding the credits for the Cellulose company and possibly other Swedish producers of cellulose have been delayed on account of completely panic like conditions in the banking world stop in order to give a hint of the conditions I want to mention that the Government of the United States only through pressure on the banks can get its need of short term credits filled. The city of New York has during a long time unsuccessfully tried to get credit stop when it finally was arranged a few days ago it was allowed under such conditions that have to be looked upon as a distress help situation through the issue of notes for one, two and three years at an interest rate of 6 percent and it was noted with great surprise when the near issue was a success stop there seem to be good prospects for a relatively fast recovery and much attention is focused on the new Reconstruction Finance Corporation which is designed to bring about a reasonable inflation.
Kreugivar

(PA)

Ivar Kreuger was to a certain extent optimistic and his belief in a recovery of the stock market in America was confirmed by a strong market in Stockholm at that particular time.

Extract from the Swedish press:
Thursday January 21st 1932, Dagens Nyheter (DN): Large Kreuger—Buying, debentures over 200 in New York

Friday January 22nd (DN): Continued Kreuger hausse on the Stock Exchange. The hausse continued from Thursday and powerful purchasing pushed up the turnover for debentures, to more that 5,000 in the beginning, and more than 8,000 for the whole day. The gains were 27:—to a high of 212. STAB gained 5:—to a high of 110:-

January 24th (DN): A weaker tendency on the market. New York market is weak.

January 26th (DN): Kreuger papers stronger again.

January 27th (DN): Continued hausse in Kreuger papers.

January 29th (DN): The Stock Market was calm and unchanged. The largest turnover was in Kreuger debentures.

Day after day the situation grew worse for those that speculated against the Kreuger Group.

On January 28th, what has been called "the Boliden Communiqué" was published.

Extract:
"The option for the Boliden shares expires at the end of January 1932 and the Board of Kreuger & Toll considers the use of this option to be a great asset to the Group. As present conditions are not suitable for a cash purchase of this size, the Group has reached an agreement through which ca 80% of the stock in Boliden's Gruv AB is acquired by means of the transfer of nom. 80,833,340 AB Kreuger & Toll participating debentures. Kreuger and Toll has reserved the right to repurchase these debentures for cash at a rate equal to the option—price at any time before December 31st 1934.

(RA)

If you look at the net profits of Boliden during the following years, up to 1938, you will see that the totals approximate or equal the purchase price. It must be considered that it was a rather interesting deal that Kreuger & Toll was offering. Another interesting thing to be observed in this communiqué is that Kreuger & Toll reserves the right to repurchase *these debentures*. This meant that they must be available at any time before December 31st 1934. In other words they could not be sold in the open market—only be used as collateral.

This in turn ought to mean that the debentures of the Boliden issue never were sold. They might have been exchanged for other debentures that earlier had been used as collateral and these old debentures were sold on the open market while the new ones were tied up number for number as new collateral. If this were to be true it would have been a tremendously smart move by Kreuger. He would have pulled out all the "old" debentures in the market where they would be available also to the short-speculators. However, to cover a short position would be next to impossible, as the new debentures were "locked in" as collateral and could not be sold freely. Unfortunately no investigation was made on this point, and any suggestions for an accounting or investigation in this matter were blocked by Marcus Sr. and Jacob Wallenberg.

The Boliden Communiqué was fairly well received in Europe, with the exception of some newspapers that, at least in the beginning, stayed somewhat neutral. Dagens Nyheter (DN) gave the following account of the communiqué:

"The rumors that for a long time have been going around Kreuger & Toll in connection with the improvement of the quotes for the Group's stocks and debentures received on Wednesday a partial explanation through a press release sent by Kreuger from New York.

Unfortunately, the release does not contain the expected information about foreign transactions which are supposed to be the reason for Mr. Kreuger's, from time to time, extended stay in the US. Possibly the extensions are a part of these negotiations." DN further mentioned some preliminary information about the Group's results and profits for 1931 and the write off on foreign Government Bonds. You are also informed that Kreuger & Toll has used its option to acquire the majority of the shares in Boliden which are liquidated through a provisional payment with Kreuger debentures with the full right to repurchase these until the end of 1934. In connection with this information the message contains one for the American public enthusiastic motivation for the acquisition of Boliden.

Kreuger's opponents were now forced to take counter action. In order to do so Dagens Nyheter published the following picture in Stockholm:

In my opinion the picture is lacking something. There should be people with well known silhouettes, in the upper part of the brook, feeding it with forged debentures or debentures from "blocked" collateral.

At the same time a Danish professor, V. Brick, was engaged and confirmed from Denmark that Boliden was completely worthless. Professor Brick admittedly lacked all knowledge what so ever with regard to mines and he had never been even close to Boliden. However, in this connection that did not seem to be of the slightest concern. Brick was a Professor with some knowledge in national economy. His statements were published and that sufficed for this type of anti Kreuger propaganda. The picture in Dagens Nyheter, as well as Brick's statements, was immediately spread all over Europe and the US through the opponents' network.

The rumors had the desired effect. The Boliden issue in America failed and had to be temporarily shelved. In addition, the promise for the acceptance credits that Kreuger had negotiated for the cellulose industries were withdrawn. Possibly, the reasons were the exceptionally nervous economical situation in the US at that moment. It is not unusual that the market is tightening 3-6 months before a bottom is reached, and you can foresee a turnaround. There is no doubt that the negative propaganda from among other places, Sweden, played an important part as a triggering factor.

The short selling was intensified.

Kreuger was not in a hurry to put Boliden on the market. He knew what he had and that there was an interest from many parties—for instance the Guggenheim's—and that these were real interests. In fact the interest was still there after his death. However, it must have been a big disappointment to run into such a well, organized opposition. Especially as the Boliden transaction was in all parts a very sound business.

The Boliden business had to be put aside for a while. There were other deals, such as the Italian match monopoly, the problems of liquidity in the Group, and loans promised to other countries that Kreuger had to deal with. Apart from these matters, Kreuger had succeeded in getting documented evidence against some of those who were acting against him. The evidence was probably in the form of forged debentures, forged certificates of deposits and such debentures that belonged to collateral that was blocked, through an agreement, and should not be possible to sell in the open market. It is also possible that he had obtained some of his own debentures that should be secured in his own vault. Someone amongst his own people could have lent them to short sellers. (Such lending was considered a help, when a short seller could not cover his sales.)

It was important that Kreuger returned to Europe and to Stockholm in order to take care of the Swedish part of the resistance, and to take legal actions at the same time, as the situation of liquidity had to be cleared up. Paris was, however, to be the first on his list for several reasons. Firstly, a legal process had already begun against certain short sellers and forgers, and secondly Paris was geographically more suitable for connections with Italy. To a large extent things now became more a question of time. Therefore, Kreuger arrived in Paris on March 11th 1932—for the last time in his life.

Ivar Kreuger died Saturday March 12th 1932.

The circumstances of his death are dealt with in the following chapter.

Boliden after the death of Ivar Kreuger

When the death of Ivar Kreuger was officially announced, disturbances, and a complete panic broke out. This was well organized by Kreuger's opponents who in fact went into action already on March 13th—the day after Kreuger's death. The Board of Kreuger & Toll was tricked into appointing a committee of investigators. Their mission, according to agreement, should be *to assist* the Board, in its work to analyze the Group's economical situation. This committee was also known as "The Royal Commission", although no such commission was ever appointed. It was, however, an impressive name. This committee consisted mainly of people opposed to Ivar Kreuger and they quickly took command over the Board of Directors, and took charge of investigations, as well as the administration. The Committee's purpose was to put Kreuger & Toll in bankruptcy and to split up the Group. All questions or attempts of reconstruction were turned down. The Group was to be split. The valuable parts were going to be taken over, and administrated by its new owners. (*read members of the Committee*).

One of the members of the committee was a young and very clever, disrespectful, and ruthless business lawyer named Hugo Stenbeck who did not hesitate to use whatever means necessary in order to reach his goals. The goals varied a little within the committee but as far as Stenbeck was concerned there was only one goal—to become rich. And one has to admit that he was quite successful in reaching that goal. Some of the other members were not far behind him, but as they represented, and owned majority shares in banks. Their goals were to make the bank in question rich.

To create the panic needed to press down the quotes on the Stock Exchange for all shares that in one way or the other were connected with the Kreuger Group, the press, mainly Dagens Nyheter continued to spread negative information. This is an old, but quite useful method. To create the necessary panic within the Group itself, other methods were used such as threats, actions by the police, threats of prison, claims for compensation, and so on. You name it and the Committee used it. All the time Hugo Stenbeck and Jacob Wallenberg (representative for Stockholms Enskilda Bank) "leaked" confidential information about the work of the committee and it was not always that important that the leaked information was correct.

The result of these actions had almost immediate effect. All of a sudden none of Ivar Kreuger's staff or colleagues knew anything at all, and was not responsible for anything. Information given one day was taken back the following day, or was completely contradicted on the third day. The Kreuger Group´s chief auditor, Mr. A Wendler gave, for example, six different versions of one and the same financial operation. Everything that possibly could be blamed on Ivar Kreuger—was blamed on Ivar Kreuger. There were always verbal orders and instructions that had been given by Ivar Kreuger no matter what they concerned.

This was exactly what the committee wanted and they now got into a position from which they could dictate everything. Some documents were to be used—some documents were not to be used. Some books and journals were going to be audited—some were not going to be audited—not even reviewed.

Let us take a look at one example. Without supporting evidence, I could tell you almost anything—couldn't I. However, I have to stick to the truth and be able to prove everything that is possible to prove. If not, people will still believe the false picture once given them. It is my aim to change this perception.

Sharp critics were aimed at Boliden—or the January communiqué, as it also was called. It was claimed that it contained misleading information and that the members of the Board possibly could be held liable for this. The reaction was quick.

"Erik Sjostrom maintained that he had had nothing what so ever to do with the creation of the communiqué. He did not know anything about it. Krister Littorin maintained that Erik Sjostrom participated in the negotiations with regard to the communiqué. Bergenstråhle maintained that it was Sjostrom that passed on the cable from Kreuger to him."

And so it went on. Actually Kreuger's cable was sent to Sjostrom. (SA Vol. 2)

How the investigators' committeé planned and worked can be seen from the following extract. This extract is from a meeting held April 25th 1932 with all the members in the investigating committee present, with the exception of Nothin. When the case of Boliden was discussed:

§4

"It was discussed which position the investigators should take regarding a possible extension of the moratorium for the estate (Ivar Kreuger's estate). Mr. Stenbeck announced that as far as he had been informed, the estate would claim owner's right to the shares in Boliden, which meant that if they were valued at the amount that Kreuger had maintained during the later part of his life it would be questionable, if a request for bankruptcy could be granted. It was also an uncertainty regarding the election of administrators, wherefore it was assigned to Mr. Browaldh to consider if a continuation of the moratorium for the estate could be suitable from an official point of view."

(TK)

Just one remark is required here. The moratorium of the personal estate was none of Mr. Stenbeck's business.

Boliden was—as shown—considered to be a very attractive corporation which one way or the other had to be saved for the banks. Everybody agreed on that. The question was in which way it was going to be done. That was a nut that required some time to crack.

The operation began with Mr. Ernfrid Browaldh (the leading man of the committeé) making the following declaration:

"During 1930 there were no new issues made within the Group, but there were strong additional increases of foreign bonds partly caused by repayment of earlier contracted loans and partly through considerable amounts of new loans. During 1931, for which year the books have not been closed and no annual report has been issued, could no authorized new issues be made. This considered, large placements were made on the market during the later part of 1931 and the beginning of 1932, by Ivar Kreuger, of new participating debentures originated from the debenture payment of nom. 80,833,340:—which Kreuger was supposed to receive as payment for the transfer of the Boliden shares to Kreuger & Toll and over which he had disposed prior to having freed the shares from the debts related to them. Of this block of debentures about 70 million are unaccounted for, including the amount of 16,000,000* that were put to Kreuger's disposal already in July 1931."

(RA)

*   see the story by Mr. Sune Schéle above

This is indeed an interesting declaration because it contains so many faults. You will notice this from the previously presented records. Either Mr. Browaldh does not know what he is talking about, or he is talking in bad faith. In my opinion, either is just as bad.

The plan was now to question, the right of the ownership of the shares and who had acquired the block of shares in Boliden—Ivar Kreuger or Kreuger & Toll? Had a legal sale through which Ivar Kreuger sold the shares to Kreuger and Toll taken place? Was it a fraudulent act—that was at least what was maintained—that the sale had taken place without Kreuger notifying the buyer that the shares were used as collateral in

Skandbanken? Furthermore, Browaldh maintains, that, the debentures in question, were not authorized by the Board of Kreuger & Toll.

As I said, there is not very much in Mr. Browaldh's declaration that agrees with what had actually happened. However, the most important thing was that the declaration served as a foundation, which gave an opportunity to question, to lie, to change, and to turn things around with the assistance of lawyers, who followed given instructions. In this way the investigators would be able to "keep the ball in the air" for quite some time. And that they did.

In order to increase the confusion the Boliden shares were listed as assets in both Ivar Kreuger's and Kreuger & Toll's estates. As a second step a quarrel began regarding the registration of the shares and on this point an agreement finally was made.

"On December 6th 1932 the following agreement was made between Ivar Kreuger's and Kreuger & Toll's bankruptcy estates that the shares in Boliden should be registered on Ivar Kreuger, but that this would not set precedence with regard to the rights to the shares, nor to the purchase price.

Signed
For Ivar Kreuger   For Kreuger & Toll
Tom Forssner, Alf Lindahl   Ernst Lyberg, Nils Brolén
Erik Stridsberg"

The quarrel about the Boliden shares continued and the parties quarreled about almost everything. There were copies of documents in one case and records in another case that one of the parties wanted to prevent the other part from getting a look at. After a while the case was ready for a court procedure and the pile of legal records grew to a considerable height. The records came to contain inquiries and reports from all sorts of people, who could possibly have had something of value to say in the Boliden affair, but also with persons that did not have very much to say. For every new application to the court, the other party would have the opportunity to rely and give his view. It took time and a lot of money was spent. The lawyers should be paid, the management of two estates should be paid, and witnesses should be paid.

Parallel to all the disputes, negotiations for the sale of Boliden continued. It was mostly the British side that was active. Other foreign companies were also interested in Boliden. However, there were other interests that were not so keen on the sale of Boliden, and the pulling of some strings, resulted in a letter from the Prime Minister (Statsministern).

The Murder of Ivar Kreuger

Extract:
"Statsministern
December 23rd 1933
"To Mr. Forssner

—

We want to underline what we have said previously that the Government can not accept any action which would endanger the Swedish influence over the company. Our wishes are that you inform the foreign interested party of these our points of view.

Very truly yours,
Per Albin Hansson

(RA)

The discussions were going on within the Government with regard to the possibilities of acquiring Boliden. The Governor of Stockholm asked for a quotation and an option for the purchase on the 12th of March 1934. But the present owners were not in a hurry and did not present an offer before June and then with an option that was valid for about three weeks. It was quite clear that there was a very limited interest in selling to the Government, and The Governor of Stockholm, Nothin took the hint which can be seen from his reply.

From the Governor of The Capital of Sweden
June 8th 1934
"To the administrators of the bankruptcy estate of Kreuger & Toll
We herewith confirm, having received your reply dated June 5th 1934 in which you, as far as AB Kreuger & Toll's estate rights are concerned, have given an offer for a block of shares in Boliden's Gruv AB. At the same time you have given an option valid only until Saturday June 30th 1934 12 o'clock noon. However, it must be well known to you that a decision from the Government's side at such short notice can not be taken. Therefore, we are forced to establish that we in your letter see evidence of unwillingness to find a common line of unity and agreement.
Stockholm June 8th 1934
Torsten Nothin, Tamm, N. Quensel

(RA)

One of the reasons for avoiding the Government was that the administrators figured with a greater profit, if the shares were sold at an official auction. Not a bigger profit for respective estates—but for the banks.

An interesting observation is that the Prime Minister addresses himself to the administrators of Ivar Kreuger's estate, and the Governor of Stockholm addresses himself to the administrators of Kreuger & Toll's estate.

An auction was held in the city of Malmö. Malmö was chosen because there it would be possible to discuss the commission, as well as the manner in which the auction should be held. Skandbanken bought the shares for 150 million crowns. However, this result was not acceptable to Wallenberg and Stockholms Enskilda Bank. They would preferably dictate the conditions of a settlement, a mission they let Johannes Hellner execute.

"January 22nd 1935
Herr J Hellner
Stockholm
    Since we today through bank director J. Wallenberg were informed, that you, for your work in connection with the coming into being of the agreement, dated December 20th 1934 between Skandinaviska Kredit AB, Kreuger & Toll's and Ivar Kreuger's estates and the Swedish Match Co would accept a fee, for our part, of five thousand (5,000) crowns we herewith ask for permission to send one to you addressed check for this amount and request to receive your receipt, as acknowledgement. We take the opportunity to express our deep gratitude for the important work you have performed in order to bring about the agreement.

Very truly yours
The Administrators of Kreuger & Toll's estate
MF HE

Mr. J. Hellner's reply was written on the management stationary of Stockholms Enskilda Bank (RA)

The agreement contained the following points. (Details of lesser interest have been left out.)
"Agreement between Skandbanken, K&T's estate, Ivar Kreuger's estate and STAB.
The Bank demands priority right in the K&T given collateral:
on the one hand 159,000 shares in Hufvudstaden, regarding this block a special agreement have been made between the Bank and K&T November 25th 1933,
on the other hand nom. $25,000,000 German Reich 6% bonds 1930,
and nom. $ 10,000,000 Hungarian bonds 1929 belonging to STAB
Collateral from IK:
On the one hand $ 42,000,000 German Reich 6% bonds 1930,
$ 21,000,000 turned over to IMCO,

$ 21,000,000 with ownership right taken over by the Bank,
Nom. £ 1,000,000 British Match belonging to STAB, and
84,000 + 703,513 Boliden

As soon as this agreement is legal and binding for the parties the Bank shall

1) return to K&T $ 3,000,000 German Bonds,
2) to K&T pay 6,930,000 in cash

K&T will refrain from any claims against the Bank with regard to the shares in Boliden.
The Bank will have the right to put to its credit the payment of Boliden against IK's
debts. STAB will pay to K&T 3,000,000 crowns.

When this agreement was signed, everybody should theoretically be happy. Especially, as
all parties—with the exception of the estates of Ivar Kreuger and Kreuger &Toll—had
made an extraordinarily good business deal. However, that was not the case. If prestige
had come into the court procedures—I do not know—but the fight continued, first
in the Lower Court and then in the Court of Appeal.

The various records that the Court assembled as a foundation for its final Judgment
amount to a bundle of about 10 inches in thickness to which can be added a fair amount
of memorandum and records of peripheral interest. I believe that the contents of the
judgment, that finally was passed, in a concentrated form will be enough for anyone
that does not have a special interest in this case. Kreuger & Toll was the plaintiff and
Ivar Kreuger's estate the defendant in this case.

Extract from the Lower Court's judgment July 30th 1935
    " . . . On account of this and as the defendant, the estate of Ivar Kreuger, has not
bothered to show that AB Kreuger & Toll or, after the company's bankruptcy May 24th
1932, the plaintiff, the mentioned company's bankruptcy estate, before the December
20th 1934, with Skandinaviska Kredit AB made agreement regarding the shares, should
have lost its right to these. The Court tries the plaintiff's claims and has come to the
decision that it is fair to the declare that plaintiff have had better right to the shares
than the defendant before and after the mentioned agreement with Kreditaktiebolaget.
The defendant shall pay the legal expenses."

(RA)

The judgment as such did not mean a thing as the parties involved had already solved
the problems they had had. My personal reaction against the judgment is the use of
the Swedish word "gittat" which means "having not bothered to . . . ." From this you
get the impression that the administrators of Ivar Kreuger's estate "could not care less"

as the case was clear already from the beginning. However, if you look in a dictionary you will find a secondary meaning of the word "gitta" which in this case would have the meaning "have not been able to". Either way, the whole court procedure was unnecessary and a settlement could have been reached much earlier. Going through all the material and the parties various explanations, you get a feeling that this was more or less a show, and an attempt to give an example of how complicated everything was that had with Ivar Kreuger to do.

Of course there was an appeal against the Lower Court's judgment. This was in fact rather meaningless as the following extract will show:

The Court of Appeal finds that the case had been concentrated to the question of which one of the two parties had the better right to the shares before and until the agreement December 20th 1934 was made.

"Kungliga Hovrätten (Court of Appeal) has taken into consideration the contents of documents and records and finds no reason to change the judgment of the Lower Court."

Possibly a layman should not question the judgment of the Court of Appeal, but to me it seems very strange that K&T has been judged to have a better right to the shares of Boliden "before and until" the agreement with Skandinaviska Kredit AB December 20th 1934. "Before" that is not very precise. How long time before? What were the records on which the judgment was based? I have not gone through every single record in detail, but I want to mention one in which Kreuger & Tolls purchase of Boliden is described in the following way:

"Approximately 80% of all the stocks in Boliden's Gruv AB were acquired through the transfer of 4,041,667 AB Kreuger & Toll debentures @ Kr. 20:-."

It is not very difficult to see how someone arrived at this figure. You simply take the total sum and divide by 20 and you get the number above. But why? In 1935/36 nobody might have thought about the face value, and Marcus Wallenberg, Sr. had previously declared that there was no idea to check, the outstanding amounts of debentures, as they had no value. But is it possible that there were gaps that had to be covered, just in case? Or was it important to get an easy explanation for large amounts that somehow were missing? That is, if anybody would dare to bring up such a question. This could however be an interesting question for future researchers. We, for one thing, now know that the above mentioned figures found among the documents in the Court of Appeal are wrong. I refer to Mr. Sune Schéle's story above.

Another document that is a bit confusing is a note covering the financial instruments pledged in connection with the agreement December 20th 1934 with Skandinaviska Kreditbanken:

"Pledged 72,000 A, 601,296 B and certificates of subscription 12,000 A and 102,217 B, together with $30,000,000 German Bonds belonging to IMCO"

There were no certificates of subscription in 1934. As noted above, Mr. Erik Sjostrom delivered all newly subscribed shares to Riksbanken on March 18th 1932. The amounts of the German Bonds do not tally.

Not that these things are any surprise to me but taken all together they will prove my point.

It is worth to observe the following facts:

1) Boliden as a company was practically free from debt in 1932
2) The price paid for the Boliden shares at the auction was almost double the amount listed in the bankruptcy act.
3) Boliden shares were listed on the Stock Exchange on the free list in 1935
4) Boliden shares were listed on the main list in 1955
5) Boliden as a concept has been proved to be a correct investment from the side of Ivar Kreuger.
6) If Ivar Kreuger had lived Boliden possibly could have been expanded together with the Guggenheim's,
7) Any confusion and trouble in connection with Boliden was mostly created after the death of Ivar Kreuger and was not any of his doings.

New York, 1932

As we have seen in the previous chapter, Ivar Kreuger was in New York at the beginning of 1932, negotiating the sale of a minor part of Boliden to the Guggenheim's. He was also going to introduce another issue of debentures for Kreuger & Toll in connection with their take over of Boliden, and he was trying to arrange, something that was called accept credits, for the Swedish cellulose industry.

There are unconfirmed rumors that Kreuger was discussing with Rockefeller the possibilities to build monopolies around petroleum products along the same concept as the design for the match monopolies. From the telegrams in the Swedish police archives you can see that Rockefeller bought large blocks of debentures and that Guggenheim expressed a genuine interest for Boliden. Finalizing these transactions seemed, as always, to be a matter of time.

It is quite clear that the Kreuger Group at this time was in a very difficult financial position—like so many other large conglomerates. In Kreuger's case it depended on the one hand, on the bad economical conditions that occurred at the same time in Europe as well as in America, and on the other hand on the baisse—and bear attacks, that were launched simultaneously against all the securities belonging to the Group. Finally Kreuger's choice to meet the attack by purchasing the Group's securities in the open market, and thus withdrawing them from the trade, was a heavy burden on the liquidity. In itself this tactic is correct, but it calls for a great liquidity and the availability of credit. The situation for the Group was not exactly improved when some countries where the Group had financial interests suspended all payments.

A baisse—and bear attack against a company and its securities (usually shares) is nothing new and has been practiced more or less as long as stock exchanges have existed. What you do is that you sell a security for delivery at a later date. Then you manipulate the market with the help of rumors and various other means that will spread negative impressions about the security in question. The result is that the prices will be lowered; sometimes, to a very large degree. When you feel that the bottom is reached or at least quite close—then you buy in order to be able to deliver what you once sold. This is a legal operation—if you follow the rules. The rules are that you in one way or the other should own the security that you sell short. You can borrow the security or you can deposit enough funds with your broker so that your transactions at all times can be covered. Sooner or later, you have to deliver what you initially sold. Now, if the attacked party buys such quantities in the market as to dry up the supply, there will be difficulties for those who sold short to cover their sale. They have to give higher bids in order to be able to buy some of the securities they need. A considerable amount of money can be lost this way. Today this part of the market is pretty well covered and controlled by the authorities. At the end of 1800's and beginning of 1900's, it was an entirely different story. Nobody checked if you had securities or funds available for this type of business. You just sold short and hoped for the best. For a small time operator it might have been o.k., but for a large financial operator it would mean a catastrophe, if he could not deliver.

Apart from buying in the open market, Kreuger used his debentures as collateral for loans, setting the conditions in such a way that when he wanted to call the loan—repay— then he should have the collateral freed—number for number—not the same amount of securities, but exactly the same securities that he once put on deposit as collateral. In this way he locked up considerable quantities of debentures. He also bought securities for future delivery—knowing there would be none available. The prices were pushed up. When you study the market from January 1932, you can see what is going on. Some quite big operators had sold debentures short on a large scale, and could now not get supplies. In order to cover their short positions they tried two ways. One was to forge debentures and/or certificates of deposits for debentures. Another was to sell the collateral that had been locked up for a loan through a contract. In either case you would face a severe jail sentence or heavy fines in case you were caught.

Some international operators were getting into a difficult situation. This was also the case for some Swedish operators working through French, Dutch, German and American brokers. Some of them had the possibility to "borrow" debentures from directors of Kreuger & Toll behind the back of Ivar Kreuger. Kreuger did not know anything about this at the time it happened. However, he did find out and secured evidence. The evidence was probably in the form of forged debentures or certificates of deposit and debentures that he knew should not be traded in the open market.

Kreuger was of course aware of the Group's liquidity crises but he also knew that this crisis would not remain forever. There were signs that the market was going to turn for the better. He was pretty sure that he would be able to sell a part of Boliden to the Guggenheim's and that this transaction would be a positive push for the debenture issue. At the same time he had begun legal procedures against some of the baisse operators in France. All these things taken together would bring rather large amounts to the Group and there was also the question of the Italian monopoly for matches where large sums already had been paid by Kreuger. This transaction should be settled at the latest on March 31st 1932.

In all, it was a question of time.

However, there were others who also realized that their future was depending on time.

As we saw in the previous chapter Dagens Nyheter published information about Boliden giving the readers the impression that it lacked all substance and simply was one of Kreuger's fantasies. The Danish professor, V. Birck, supported similar information without knowing what he was talking about. To him it did not matter. He was paid.

The sale of all types of Kreuger securities increased and the final negotiations regarding an agreement with Guggenheim's was postponed. But the interest remained—even after the death of Ivar Kreuger.

Kreuger also had a disagreement with Morgan regarding LM Ericsson. An agreement had been made wherein the parties should somehow exchange interests in order to avoid future competition. Morgan paid Kreuger $11 million for a block of shares in LM Ericsson and Kreuger was to buy a block of shares in ITT. All of a sudden Morgan maintained that Kreuger had given him wrong information about the financial position of LM Ericsson and therefore demanded repayment of the $11 million. An immediate reaction was of course—why did Morgan not check the finances in connection with the purchase? This could have been done within days from signing the agreement. Anyway—Kreuger did not have $11 million in cash. He had used the sum that he received for international loans. The result of the disagreement was that Kreuger had to agree to repurchase LM Ericsson and he used whatever funds he could make available at short notice for a down payment. No doubt this did not improve the liquidity of the Group.

I have heard an explanation for this disagreement that could be true but it needs further investigation. LM Eriksson's balance sheet should—in Swedish—have stated "Cash, bank and claims" and a certain figure. The translation to English is supposed to have read "Cash and bank claims". The various figures as such were correct.

Another article published in Dagens Nyheter informed the public that Ivar Kreuger had had a nervous break down in New York and that he among other things was suffering from hallucinations.

The quotations for all Kreuger securities fell to new lows.

Did Kreuger really have a nervous break down? It is possible—but there might also be a natural explanation for the behavior that has been described, without necessarily any connection to a nervous break down. It is possible that the reasons were not known in 1932. Kreuger had fallen sick with malaria during an earlier visit to either, Mexico,

Central America or Africa. This is nothing extraordinary—on the contrary—quite common. But we also know that he had a severe cold—possibly the flu—while in New York. It is not at all uncommon that you in connection with the flu—when the body's immune defense is low—get what is known as a malaria relapse giving, among other symptoms, hallucinations. You believe that you hear things, such as a knock on the door, or a telephone that rings, etc. The same effect can occur if you have been completely without sleep during a long time.

The publicity and the spreading of rumors resulted in even lower quotes, and sales of Kreuger securities increased. Attacks on a company in this way are—as mentioned above—nothing new. It has been practiced in America from the middle of the 1850th—if not earlier. It is said that, at the time of Ivar Kreuger's death, debentures for not less than 500 million had been sold—short. Unfortunately there is no information available what these 500 million represents—face value, subscription rate or average daily quotes. It does not make any difference, as the sum represents more than was available on the market. Based on the face value it would mean that twice as much had been sold, than had ever been issued. The truth is probably somewhere in the middle, which would mean close to the same amount that originally had been issued—220 million Swedish Crowns.

Ivar Kreuger's purchase of the Group's debentures on the open market has been described as a loosing proposition. This is of course not so. The prices at which he bought were considerably lower than the subscription prices and if and when the market recovered to a more normal level the profits would be quite substantial. Some of his critics call this "support buying", but that does not give the whole picture. True—it worked as support but that is not the whole picture. The buying made it possible to withdraw debentures from the market and tie them into firm collateral agreements.

I think that it is worth to remind the reader of the fact that Ivar Kreuger now was aware of what was going on behind his back. He had collected enough evidences for a court trail against his opponents in Sweden, France, Holland and America. The judgments from such trials could be very painful for his opponents. Kreuger had also given instructions for a complete audit of the Group's businesses by a completely detached firm of certified public accountants, and he had asked the Group's own accountants to go through all transactions and have them traced in detail. This action was taken by Kreuger in order to uncover any irregularities that might exist within the Group.

Unfortunately, all the material of evidence disappeared in connection with what became known as "The Investigation".

It would have been a rather simple matter to get a clear picture of all transactions that had been made in the Group's securities—especially in debentures. The investigators could have called for a complete listing of all collateral in which debentures was a part. If they were not to full satisfaction, the debt should receive the value "0" and the lenders be brought to court. Those who had lent debentures from Kreuger & Toll vaults should have to pay the full amount. I am quite sure that the documents of bankruptcy would have had a completely different look, if this had been done. That is, if it had been at all possible to declare Kreuger& Toll in bankruptcy.

Why was this not done? Mr. Wallenberg Sr. declared that as the debentures lacked any value, it would be a waste of time and effort to ask for accounts. It was as easy as that to get rid of that problem.

Some authors have accused Ivar Kreuger of holding the complete book keeping and all records of transactions in his head. Consequently, there should have been neither bookkeeping records, or accounts available. This is of course not true. What is true, however, is that he kept a special notebook, for his own private use, over transactions made as well as transactions booked in the various companies of the Group and planned transactions in connection with the year end balance sheet, etc. These notebooks, that also contained information about secret deposits and secret registrations of companies, were removed shortly after his death. First as late as in 1958 was it established in court, that the lawyer Hugo Stenbeck, admittedly removed these notebooks, used them and then destroyed them. The crime was at that time (1958) barred by the statute of limitation. The record of this event was found in the Court's archive (Ä 32/1957 Aktbil. 7) and the lawyer questioning Mr. Stenbeck at the time, has been interviewed by me.

By spreading the information that the bookkeeping was out of order—the field was opened for a "reconstruction" of the Groups accounts. The certified public accountants did not perform a good job and were (partially paid by Kreuger's opponents), and took their orders and instructions from them. Today we also have the information that some of the people in Kreuger & Toll did not always follow the instructions they had been given. Possibly "forgot" them, did not understand them or misinformed each other on purpose. As the Group consisted of roughly 160 different companies the world over, there were bound to be differences that had to be corrected. When the investigators however, did not understand a transaction or could not locate the securities at once, they did not bother with further work, but simply declared such assets as fictitious.

A serious investigation and administration with the help of Ivar Kreuger's notebooks would probably have been able to bring forward a correct—or at least a more correct—result than what was presented in the end.

Paris In March 1932

I am about to give you a lot of details and information that you might believe to be unimportant. But I assure you, they are of importance when it comes to following Ivar Kreuger and his doings, more or less step by step, until his death. This will clarify what may have occurred or rather what could not have happened.

Ivar Kreuger arrived in France by the luxury steamship "Ile de France" from New York, on Friday March 11th 1932. It was a dreary, drizzling morning when the boat train at about ten thirty pulled in at the Lazar station in Paris. Kreuger was met by the train by his CEO for the Swedish Match Company, Krister Littorin. Littorin was an old friend and they had worked together for more than 30 years. Together they took a taxi to Kreuger's apartment at 5 Avenue Victor Emanuel III (the name has now been changed to Avenue Roosevelt). During this short trip Littorin observed that Kreuger, apart from a slight paleness, was very much himself. No signs of any illness.

When Kreuger had settled in, Mr. Sune Schéle, another director from STAB arrived and the three of them were having lunch together discussing the business of the Group from various angles. It was mostly Littorin and Schéle that talked about the latest news and Kreuger who listened. The discussion was interrupted three times by incoming phone calls. One was from the Group's representative, Erik Lundberg in Rome, the second came from Ivar Kreuger's brother, Torsten in Stockholm, and the third was from Donald Durant the representative of the American banking firm Lee Higginson Co.

In order to be able to judge the pattern of Ivar Kreuger's behavior we have to know a little about the above mentioned phone calls. Mr. Lundberg wanted a meeting in Rome but Kreuger told him that he was going to Berlin on Sunday, and suggested that Lundberg should come to Paris the following Thursday which was decided. The last days of March a Board meeting was going to be held in Italy concerning the Italian monopoly for matches so there were quite a few things to be discussed regarding this matter.

The second phone call from Kreuger's brother is quite important. Kreuger was asked if he needed any form of financial assistance. Ivar said, no thank you, but admitted that it had been a period of difficulties, but that he had collected all evidence he needed and was having all the trumps on hand. Further that he had to come to Stockholm as soon as possible to settle matters and then return to Paris and New York. When the phone call came, Littorin had left the room. Schéle was the only person, with the exception of Torsten Kreuger, that now knew that Ivar Kreuger had got evidence against those who acted against him on various fronts, and that he was prepared to take action.

The third phone call came from Donald Durant and they agreed to hold a meeting at 11 o'clock at Durant's hotel the following day.

After the phone calls Kreuger, Littorin and Schéle continued their talks until 2 p.m. when four additional persons from Kreuger & Toll joined them. Schéle left when this new group arrived. It would have been extremely interesting to know, with whom Mr. Schéle spoke during the following 48 hours. Unfortunately so far no such information has been uncovered.

The new meeting lasted until 3.45 p.m., when Kreuger and Littorin had to break for another meeting at 4.00 p.m., in Hotel Maurice where they were to meet with Oscar Rydbeck, director of Skandinaviska Banken, which was the Group's main banking connection in Sweden. Oscar Rydbeck was also a member of the Board of Kreuger & Toll. Kreuger and Littorin took a taxi to the hotel.

This meeting lasted until 6.00 p.m. Rydbeck kept a diary and noted Kreuger's arrival at 4.00 p.m. and that he and Littorin left the hotel at 6.00 p.m. Another notation of certain interest shows that Kreuger reacted negatively when he was informed that Mr. Bergenstråhle from the Investment Department of Kreuger & Toll also had come to Paris. Bergenstråhle was in charge of the Investment Department and had in his care all new issues, all securities and all debentures and other securities that Kreuger had been buying. Bergenstråhle was also responsible for the communication between Kreuger & Toll and all its financial connections in various parts of the world. To this I can add a new piece of information received through research at the Riksarkiv. All outgoing information from Kreuger & Toll as well as from Ivar Kreuger himself passed through the Investment Department.

Littorin left Kreuger outside his apartment at approx. 6.20 p.m. Littorin was going to have dinner with the representatives from Lee, Higginson & Co and Kreuger wanted to make an early night, as he claimed to be a bit tired—and expected a visit from a woman.

We have now—without too many details—covered the whole day of Friday March 11th 1932, more or less, hour for hour, and we can see that Ivar Kreuger has not been alone at any time. All meetings, phone calls and the time is well documented and verified. Why is this so important? Because, at roughly 5.00 p.m. a pistol was bought by a man, who said his name was Ivar Kreuger.

The Purchase Of The Gun

Sometime between 4.00 and 5.00 p.m. on Friday March 11th a man who said his name was Ivar Kreuger entered the gun shop of Gastinne Renette in order to buy a weapon. How do we know that? By the statements in a police hearing with Antoine Bervillier who served this customer. How can we be sure of the timing? According to law, all sales will have to be registered in a special book. This particular sale is entered on page 165 as number 45 and after that there are an additional 17 entered sales the same day. The last sale entered was registered on page 176. With the support of these notes it is established that 5.00 p.m. would be the last time possible for this sale to be entered.

Where was Ivar Kreuger at around 5.00 p.m.? Ivar Kreuger and Littorin were in a meeting with Oscar Rydbeck between 4.00 and 6.00 p.m., which has been well established. This proves that Ivar Kreuger could not have been the man that bought the pistol. Consequently, the man who did buy the pistol was not Ivar Kreuger but someone else.

The man who bought the weapon was according to the salesman around 40 years of age. When he was asked what kind of weapon he wanted he answered immediately—a revolver—after having been shown two revolvers of different caliber he shrugged his shoulders as if it was just the same, if it was going to be a revolver or a pistol. It is true that it does not matter very much, if you are shot, or if you shoot yourself with a revolver or a pistol. It is the result that counts. From a criminal investigation point it is very important to distinguish the two weapons. In this particular case the customer hesitated for a moment in the choice of revolver or pistol and finally made up his mind to buy a pistol. The first offered was of caliber 6.35 and 7.65 but they were obviously too small. A Browning of caliber 9 mm was immediately accepted. The buyer asked for a demonstration of the weapon. He wanted to know how to load it. When asked if he wanted a box with 25 cartridges he asked to get 4 boxes, that is 100 cartridges. The pistol and a pamphlet were packed in a green carton and the salesman asked if he should put the cartridges in the same package. "No, I will take them in my pocket", replied the buyer. In the journal where all sales were registered, the name and address of the customer also had to be noted. When asked about his name, the buyer spelled it out I-v-a-r K-r-e-u-g-e-r. He paid cash.

If you want to maintain that it was Ivar Kreuger who was the buyer you will first have to explain how he could be in two different places at the same time. In a meeting with two other persons and at the same time enter a shop in order to buy a weapon. There are some other peculiarities. Ivar Kreuger was a very good marksman and an owner of at least a dozen handguns, which can be seen from the estate inventory. There would have been no need for him to ask for a demonstration. Another thing—why buy 100 cartridges? If you intend to kill yourself you will hopefully only need one and in the worse case, two bullets. I would not say anything if there only were boxes containing 100 each, but to buy 3 extra boxes which never were going to be used does not seem very clever. And why separate the cartridges from the gun, and take them in the coat pocket? They do weigh some 750 gram and do not exactly improve the look of a coat. Finally, it is difficult to imagine Ivar Kreuger, with a loud voice spell out his name, when he, under all other circumstances, never wanted to mention his own name or wanted it to appear on any official documents, such as passenger lists, or in connection with ordering a theatre ticket, etc.

The knowledge of the details in connection with the death of Ivar Kreuger seems to have been forgotten. Some journalists claim that he committed suicide in a hotel room in Paris. When asked of the name of the hotel they can of course not give you a reply. They write about something that they in fact do not know anything—or at least very little—about. And they do not want to do any research either. Some will tell you that Kreuger shot himself in the heart; others will tell you that he shot himself in the head, and sometimes it was with a revolver and sometimes with a pistol. They do not seem to know the difference. As there is so much contradictory information in circulation it seems to be a good idea to bring a little order into the case.

First of all Ivar Kreuger was found in his own apartment more precisely to the left on a double bed in his own bedroom. The weapon that might have been used was a pistol (not a revolver) of the Browning brand with a caliber of 9 mm.

The information that Ivar Kreuger was found in a hotel room can be connected to the Russian Author Ilja Ehrenburg, who roughly half a year earlier had published a book about a Swedish Match King, who dies in a hotel room in Paris. (The Russians have had excellent timing when it comes to books of this type. It is said that they published another book about a Swedish statesman, who got shot in the open street—Prime Minister Olof Palme. This book was also published before the killing happened.)

—

Some readers may not know the difference between a revolver and a pistol and for that reason this might be the right place to give some additional information about the two types of weapon.

The revolver Fig.1 has a magazine that usually holds 6 cartridges. The name revolver associates to something that rotates and it is the magazine that moves one move for each shot fired. The empty shells remain in the magazine and have to be removed manually in exchange for new ones when all six shots have been fired. Of course nothing prevents you from replacing only one cartridge when a shot has been fired. On a modern weapon you can replace the whole magazine and quickly replace it with a new and fully loaded. The reloading of the old magazine can then be done at a convenient time.

Fig 2 shows a pistol of a little smaller and different type than what might have been used in the Kreuger case. As can be seen from the picture the pistol has its magazine in the butt. The magazine is loaded by pushing down the cartridges in the cassette, which in turn is pushed into the butt. The cassette has a spring in the bottom, which pushes up the cartridges as they are fired. The upper part of the pistol—the casing—is moveable. In order to make the pistol ready to fire you move the casing back and then forward again. This allows one cartridge to move from the magazine and into the barrel or chamber ready to be fired at the same time as the mainspring is set. Some pistols are fitted with a hammer that can be manually set.

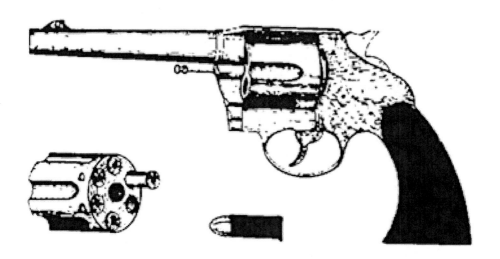

Fi7g. 1 Revolver

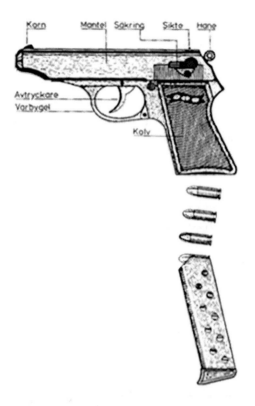

Fig.2 Pistol

I am a layman when it comes to guns and the above description could probably have been made much better, but I hope that it is clear enough and that the pictures will make you understand roughly how it works.

Now comes an important part.

When a shot is fired—it does not matter if it is with a revolver or a pistol—several things will happen (apart from that it goes "bang"—which it does most of the time). Let us start with the revolver. When a shot is fired the magazine automatically moves one click clockwise which makes it ready to fire the next shot. The empty shell remains in the magazine. The gas from the gunpowder, which appears in connection with the explosion when the shot is fired, will partly follow the bullet through the barrel while other parts will be forced backwards and will be pushed out around the magazine. These gases contain microscopic particles of soot and other products of combustion. These particles

84

will settle on the shooter's hand usually on the thumb, index—and middle fingers. In some cases it can also settle on the ring finger and the hand itself (see picture). This makes it fairly simple for a police detective to decide if a suspect or a person that has committed suicide actually had held the gun when the shot was fired.

It is a little bit different when you fire a pistol. Part of the powder gas follows the bullet through the barrel in the same way as with the revolver. The gases that are forced backwards fill another and very important function. The powder gases move the casing, which means several things. The empty shell is thrown out (most of the time on the right side of the gun), at the same time that the microscopic gas particles settles in the shooters thumb grip, and a new cartridge goes into the chamber, and the hammer or mainspring is set which makes the gun ready to fire again. You can fire, shot after shot, through pressing the trigger without reloading until the magazine is empty. That is why a weapon like this is called half-automatic.

The weapon that was found together with Ivar Kreuger's body was, as mentioned earlier, a pistol of the brand Browning with a caliber of 9 mm. This gun has a small specialty. The backside of the butt has to be held in a firm grip, as it has to be pressed into the butt in order to release the firing mechanism. As a layman you can say that the Browning has an extra safety device. If the grip is not firm enough you can not fire the weapon. A gun of this type is fairly heavy, roughly 900 grams, that is close to 2 pounds. In this particular case it was loaded with three cartridges (97 were found in their respective cartons).

If you fire the gun at a distance nothing much happens with the gases that follow the bullet through the barrel. However, if you fire a shot at a very close distance, a contact shot or attached shot a few things of interest occur.

Let us assume that we are dealing with a contact shot where the bullet penetrates a shirt before entering the body. When the bullet, and the powder gases that follows the bullet, leaves the barrel, some of it will follow the bullet, while the rest will spread in a characteristic pattern, which will stick around the penetration hole in the fabric. Furthermore, you will find a cross-formed splitting and possibly also powder burns. But one more very important thing happens. When the gases leave the barrel they create a vacuum. Nature does not like vacuum but will fill it as soon as possible. In this case the barrel will for a very short moment act as a powerful vacuum cleaner. The force of suction is quite strong and the powder gases will return. As they have been spreading somewhat they will stick to the fabric around the penetration hole, but this time from the underside. This happens in all cases with a contact shot. It is nicer however to describe what is happening when a shot has been fired through a shirt rather than through the bare skin. If the bullet should penetrate an additional article of clothing such as for example an under shirt or under west it would probably also show signs of powder burns.

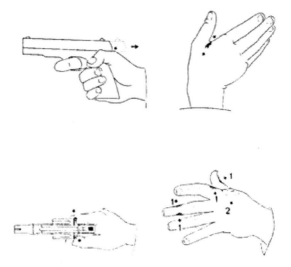

Fig. 3 Upper—shows powder traces in the thumb grip when a pistol is used. Lower—shows powder traces on fingers and hand when a revolver is used.

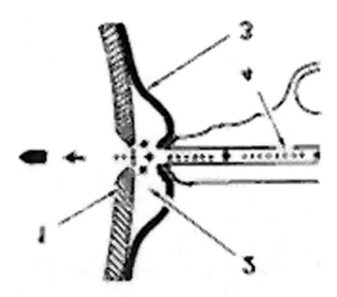

Fig. 4 Contact shot. 1). Shows penetration. 2). Shows powder gases, powder soot, and burn damages. 3). Inside after a cross formed split (textiles etc). 4. Shows the re-sucking.

The Murder of Ivar Kreuger

A forensic technician and a medico-legal practitioner can rather quickly establish a correct picture of what has happened in connection with for instance a murder. *If,* everything in a case points at the possibility of a contact shot, but at the same time the characteristic traces of the powder gases are missing, then it is quite probable that *someone,* for some reason, is trying to hide, what actually happened.

This seems to be the right place to mention the investigations of suicide with handguns made by Dr. Olle Lindquist and his collaborators at the Institute of Forensic Medicine in Uppsala. On an average there are 1,580 cases of suicide in Sweden per year. Only a minor part is committed with handguns. Of the 348 cases investigated, 66 persons had used a revolver or a pistol. 58 of these persons used a shot against the head. Only in 8 cases had the shot been aimed against the body, and then mostly at the left side of the chest. It is clearly not as easy as one might believe to commit suicide, as one of the 8 shot himself in the shoulder. The survival rate was as high as 39.3%. The average survival rate is 20%. Women usually aim for a shot against the body, while men usually aim for the head.

From the above mentioned investigation, it can be seen that a shot aimed at the heart is not too commonly used—only in about 10% of all cases—and that not all attempts are successful. We should not try to get something else out of this investigation.

Fig. 3
   Above, shows how the soot particles from the powder gases settle on the hand of the shooter when using a pistol. Below shows the same thing when a revolver is used.

Fig. 4
   Illustrates what happens in connection with a contact shot. 1) The penetration 2) Shows where powder burns and soot particles are found 3) Shows the inside which first has received a cross formed split. 4) Shows how the powder gases are sucked back into the barrel.

Let us leave the details in connection with the purchase of the pistol as well as the technical description and return to the actual case of the death of Ivar Kreuger.

(The illustrations are from The National Swedish Police Board's book of instructions)

—

Ivar Kreuger spent the evening of Friday March 11th and the night together with the woman that he had planned should come to fill an important role in his future life. They had their supper together in Kreuger's apartment, sat in front of the fire and talked for several hours. Talked about what? They talked about life, about the existence, and about their future. They had talked about the apartment that he had furnished and decorated for her. She had been very happy and Kreuger was very happy. They agreed to go together to see the new apartment at Place Vendome on Sunday morning, in order to see what the architects had accomplished, before Kreuger had to go to Berlin.

According to her own statements she had been a little worried before she met Kreuger, as she had been informed that he had been ill. She expected to find him tired as well as depressed. Her fears were not confirmed—on the contrary—Ivar Kreuger had been both happy and calm and they had spent a very nice evening together.

Paris Saturday March 12th 1932

Saturday March 12th 1932 was the day for the funeral ceremony of the great French politician and statesman Aristide Briand. Quite a few of the large streets in the center of Paris had been closed off from traffic for the cortege.

Ivar Kreuger's female visitor left around 8 a.m. and Kreuger had his breakfast alone around 8.30-9 a.m. As agreed, Krister Littorin was to visit Kreuger in the morning in order to report from the previous evening's dinner with the American bankers. This would also allow them to discuss any news that might have reached the Group during the night. As the main streets were closed Littorin arrived at Avenue Victor Emanuel III nr. 5a, little delayed, around 9.30. He observed that Kreuger was not fully dressed but dressed in a smoking jacket, which gave him the opinion that Kreuger had been a late riser.

Littorin talked and Kreuger listened—with a remark every now and then. The reporting went on until 9.55 a.m. when Miss Karin Bokman (Ivar Kreuger's private secretary stationed in Stockholm) arrived. It has not been possible to get any form of statement with regard to why Miss Bokman came to Paris. Unconfirmed information says that it was Krister Littorin—on suggestion from bankdirector Rydbeck—who had ordered her to go to Paris. Kreuger had not asked her to come—on the contrary—he had from New York sent her a certain amount of money and a private letter (content of which is unknown). According to information given to me by Torsten Kreuger's wife Diana Kreuger, Miss Bokman was very fond of Ivar Kreuger and jealous of the woman whom he planned to marry. The letter could simply have been a discreet notice of termination. This information must however be accepted for what it is. But there is no motivation for or other information regarding just why Miss Bokman came to Paris. However, if she had not come, events could definitely have taken a turn for the better.

Krister Littorin left the apartment a few minutes past 10. When he is leaving he asks Miss Bokman to remind Kreuger of the meeting (with Durant and others) which she promised to do. At 10.45 a.m. Miss Bokman prepares to leave the apartment, but just before she leaves, Kreuger complains of a sudden, severe, fatigue. He follows her to the door and she reminds him of the meeting. He replies that he will just make himself ready to leave. At 10.45 a.m. the housekeeper, Miss Barrault, also leaves the apartment. It has not been possible to find out if the parties saw each other at this time. A few minutes before 11, a telegram arrives. At that time Kreuger is fully dressed and seems to be prepared to leave for the meeting (witness: the boy that delivered the telegram—the last one to see Kreuger alive—apart from the murderer). Strangely enough there is no specific information available about this delivery boy. You would have expected some sort of police hearing. Strangely, the original telegram has not been found, nor a copy of the original. Potentially, such material could exist in the archives of STAB, which strangely enough are closed to research. Why?

At 12.10 p.m. the housekeeper Miss Barrault is back. She is very exact with time—she is leaving at 10.45 and returns at 12.10. She has been out shopping in order to be able to fix lunch (but this is not her ordinary shopping time according to research done by a French journalist). The telephone rings with a request to speak with Ivar Kreuger. According to the information given by Miss Barrault to the police, she goes to find Kreuger. In fact she has given two versions of her actions. In one she maintains that she has looked through the keyhole, in the other that she opened the door just a crack and in both cases she had seen Kreuger asleep on his bed. She said that she went back to the phone and told the caller that Kreuger was asleep *and could not be disturbed.*

At a first glance there seems to be no reason to question the statements given to the police by Miss Barrault. It could possibly even be considered to be quite a logical action.

(This far information can be verified by documents in the police archives at the City Archives in Stockholm)

At the hotel where the meeting was going to take place, they began to worry. It was not uncommon that Ivar Kreuger was late for a meeting and in this particular case he had given a warning that he might be 10-15 minutes late. Could there be a last minute, private, meeting in his apartment? Someone that wanted to make sure that he would be in his apartment at a certain time? Nobody knows why he expected to be a little late.

At 11.30 a.m. a call was made from the hotel to Kreuger's apartment. The call was answered by a male voice informing them, that Kreuger was out and not at home. One hour later the group decided that Littorin and Miss Bokman should take a taxi to Kreuger's apartment to find out what was going on.

When they arrived at the apartment and asked Miss Barrault where Kreuger was, she replied that he was asleep and slept so heavily that he did not even hear the telephone ring.

Littorin entered Kreuger's bedroom. It should be observed that Mr. Littorin is the first witness that found Kreuger. Ivar Kreuger lay on the left side of the bed flat on his back.

His coat and waistcoat were unbuttoned and folded to the left. In the vicinity of the heart a small hole could be seen. In his left hand Kreuger was holding—in a cramped grip—an automatic pistol. (These are Littorin's own words). Littorin said that there was also something odd with Kreuger's position, that he could not put his finger on. He asked all his friends to remember exactly what he had told them, no matter what happened to Littorin himself. Littorin has stuck to this, his first impression, throughout the years.

My research has confirmed that Kreuger was right handed. But it has also confirmed that his left index finger (trigger finger) was one joint short and stiff from an accident when he was young.

After Littorin, Miss Bokman and Miss Barrault entered the room. Miss Bokman, when heard by the police, stated that she seemed to remember (her memory was very short at that time) that on the left side of the body, close to the half opened hand there had been a pistol. Miss Barrault gives roughly the same testimony. The estimated time of the death of Ivar Kreuger can be set to some time around 11-11.30 a.m.

Of course, it was decided to call in the police. At first Mr. Littorin and Miss Bokman went together to the police station, but as they had to wait for quite some time, they split up. Unfortunate circumstances made Miss Bokman the reporter to the police. And in her report she only maintains that her boss, Ivar Kreuger, had committed suicide (possibly that he had shot himself). Based upon this report the French police establish its actions. It is on this report that a certain Josef Sachs bases a story that he later presents to journalists. And it is also on this report that those who maintain that Ivar Kreuger committed suicide base their opinions. In fact, it is only one person that from the beginning says that Kreuger shot himself—Miss Karin Bokman—and it is easy to understand that she—especially at the moment in question—did not know what she was talking about. Everyone that during all the years from 1932 has believed in the theory of suicide has been building their beliefs on the words of Miss Bokman. Amazingly, this also applies to the police.

Mr. Littorin returned to the hotel and the waiting meeting members in order to report what has happened, and to contact the Kreuger family. At this meeting it is decided not to make Kreuger's death official until after the close of the Stock Exchanges in Europe and the US. This action is important to keep in mind because someone seems to have known about Kreuger's death and that "someone" worked together with brokers. Very large amounts of Kreuger securities were thrown into the market just before or at about the time that Kreuger died. I have managed to locate and decode some interesting telegrams, which have never been read before. They prove this point, and if you read on, you will know who did it.

Around 3 p.m. the police arrived at Kreuger's apartment. There is no investigation made, worth the name. It is recorded that the gun is at Kreuger's left side and left hand as described by the witnesses. It is also recorded that the pistol had been loaded with three cartridges. One was fired and the empty shell was found on the floor to the right of Kreuger. Another version of the same report says that the empty shell was found beside the dead body.

This is of course not a correct statement. The officer is giving right/left indications for the empty shell from the way he himself is standing. If you base an investigation on this method the left/right positions will change whenever the investigator himself is turning. The empty shell is of course to the left of Kreuger—on the floor—where it should be. Also the statement "next to the dead body" for the position of the shell is wrong. You would expect a police report to be more exact. Furthermore—and I think that this is rather important—the police does not record the impression from the first-hand witness Mr. Littorin. His statements have been removed from all reports.

The report continues with the other cartridges. One was found in the magazine and one was found in the barrel (chamber). This becomes a little tricky. In the police report translated from French to Swedish the cartridge in the chamber is lost—it is not mentioned among the items removed for registration. On the other hand in the French report of registered items the cartridge in the magazine is lost. One must come to the conclusion that either there is something fishy here or also that it is a result of a very poor job. It could however mean that for some reason one cartridge has not been accounted for and someone tries to cover this fact. I do not want to "create" something that does not exist but at the same time I do not want anything to be overlooked and there are definitely reasons for being extremely critical in this particular case.

About 3.30 p.m. the police physician arrives and quickly comes to the conclusion that Kreuger is dead. The doctor's report contains the following statements:

"The death seems to have been caused by a bullet from the pistol found next to the body. There was a bullet-hole a couple of centimeters to the right of Kreuger's left breast. The bullet had possibly penetrated the heart or an artery causing an instant death. There seemed to have been a considerable amount of blood on Kreuger's back (he was flat on his back on a soft bed). There was no exit hole. There was no bullet hole in either the coat or the waistcoat as they had been folded to the left side. However, there were some bloodstains on the inside of the waistcoat. (?) The bullet had penetrated the shirt leaving a ragged hole, stained with burned powder and blood. The undershirt was penetrated showing a small round hole with bloodstains."

Now, a ragged hole could very well be a bad translation by someone not knowing how to describe the characteristic look of a bullet hole in a textile material. Nor were the powder stains described in any other way than saying that the edges of the hole in the shirt were blackened by burning powder. You would have expected something better from a police report. However, what is more important is that nothing is mentioned about powder stains on the inside of the textiles as would be expected from the returning powder gases after a shot. Maybe there were no such stains. You might not get the characteristic pattern from gunpowder on the penetrating side neither any traces on the inside of the textiles if the gun is held at a distance. But in such a case you could not be sure about exactly where the bullet would hit—could you?

The doctor continues his report by saying that he is not able to follow the entrance of the bullet into the body and that there was no hole showing where the bullet should have left the body. The doctor recommended an autopsy.

It is worth noting that the apartment was left empty (apart from the body), and apart from Miss Barrault during a certain time, between approx. 1.30 p.m. and 3.00 p.m.

As far as I know there are no definite supports for the theory of suicide—oral or written. Possibly you could refer to economical reasons but as all material is not available and no material guaranteed not to have been manipulated is available, it is indeed very difficult to get an opinion of what things would look like if Kreuger had lived. An analysis of Kreuger's pattern of behavior does not give an impression of an approaching suicide situation. Neither does the letters that have been called the farewell letters. I will discuss these later.

I have gone through all available material, including the police records, innumerable times. Every time I reach the conclusion that something is wrong. Small details, but nevertheless, there is something wrong. Let us take a look at some of them.

The French police give a lot of details about Kreuger's clothes. Holes, powder stains, blood stains etc. The police removed the clothes and took them to the police station in order to make a thorough inspection. Among other things police noted bloodstains on the inside of the waistcoat. How could that be? The coat and the waistcoat had been folded to the side and there were no bloodstains on the coat or in the vicinity of the waistcoat. From where did these bloodstains come? A body flat on its back sheds very little—if any—blood through a bullet hole in the chest. The bleeding goes mostly inwards.

Miss Barrault arrived at the police station in the evening of the 12th with a brochure showing various hand guns saying that she found the material in the inside pocket of Kreuger's overcoat when she was looking for his keys. The brochure had been packed with the gun. If Kreuger unpack the gun, why would he put the brochure in the inside pocket of his over-coat? Isn't it extremely unlikely that he ever carried his keys in the inside pocket of his over-coat. Finally, what business did Miss Barrault have with Kreuger's keys? Could she have been looking for the key to a safe? (MH)

93

In Kreuger's apartment various unidentified people moved around. Documents were collected and packed. Documents were burned. All rooms were carefully searched for material that could be of interest. There are no lists covering this "inventory". A considerable amount of the documents were packed and sealed in suitcases that were taken to Stockholm. In spite of this careful search of the apartment Miss Barrault turns up once again at the police station with the four cartons of cartridges—that is with the 97 still remaining in the cartons—which she said she found in Kreuger's wardrobe. There is no record of Miss Barrault having been questioned in connection with these finds.

My question is: "Is it probable that with all the people searching the apartment, they would all miss the four cartons with ammunition in the wardrobe?" A wardrobe at that era would have been a logical place for keeping documents, and a small safe. The police asked no questions.

In March 1933—almost exactly one year after the death of Ivar Kreuger, the Swedish police made an investigation in order to prove that it was Ivar Kreuger that was the person found dead in his apartment in Paris.

Let us summarize what we know so far. The investigations—the French and the Swedish—if they now should be called investigations—are filled with incorrect information. The type of weapon varies. The times given are wrong. When the Swedish investigation is made, some of the faults of the French investigation are corrected. Again you must ask the question: Is this just an example of a very poor job, or are the two investigations just a manipulated farce?

These facts are available in police reports and records, such as the Physicians' Report, police hearings with Littorin, Bokman, Barrault, the man who sold the gun, the concierge of the apartment building.

The question is now—was it a suicide or a murder?

Let us again review some facts:

Kreuger is found on his back on his bed with coat and waistcoat unbuttoned and folded to his left side with both his arms stretched along his sides. A pistol was found, on his left side close to the half opened left hand. (We will for a moment, forget Mr. Littorin's first hand impression that Kreuger was holding the gun in a cramped grip in his left hand).

Question 1: Is it possible to take a fairly heavy gun (about. 675 grams), in the right hand (Kreuger was right handed) and hold it in such a firm grip, required to make it possible to fire, point it at the heart, (requires quite a hard twist of the wrist) and pull the trigger. Could the recoil have the effect that it throws the gun to the *left* in such a way that it comes to rest on the left side of the body close to the left hand, with barrel and butt in right direction? The space between the body and the side of the bed is rather narrow.

I have spoken to Criminal Investigators, to gun experts and to physicians and they conclude that the above is impossible. Well, if Ivar Kreuger could not have shot himself with the gun in his right hand, there are not too many alternatives.

Question 2: Could the right handed Kreuger have shot himself with the gun in the left hand and got it to remain in the hand (as Littorin says) when the left arm comes to rest along the left side of the body? The gun got out of the grip, at a light touch of the hand

The experts once more say no—it is not possible. This statement was made when we did not even know that Kreuger's left "trigger finger" was stiff and one joint short, which of course makes it even more impossible. We may here have an explanation for Littorin's expression "cramped grip". If the gun has been pressed into Kreuger's hand but the index finger could not be used in the grip, then it might very well have looked as "a cramped grip".

We also have the problem with the three cartridges. It is believed that three were used as the remaining 97 of the 100 in the boxes were found. One shot was fired and the empty shell found on the floor. One cartridge was found by the police, in the magazine, and they claim that they also found one in the "chamber". But what happened to it? In order to get it out you have to make a "loading movement". Who did that? The police? If you have physically handled the weapon and plundered the chamber it should hardly be possible that one of the two cartridges just would disappear. It was not registered and did not receive a seal as all the other items that the police documented.

Could the police have made an error in their thinking? They knew that a shot was fired; it is noted that there is a cartridge in the magazine; therefore, it should also have been one in the "chamber". This reasoning is logical—it ought to have been a cartridge also in the "chamber"—and that is what they write. It is also worth noting that it is the same police officer that empties the weapon and that writes the report but does not register the cartridge in question. The registration took place Sunday March 13th 1932—the day after the pistol was found. The Swedish police records made in 1933 were adjusted on this point compared with what the police wrote in 1932.

Let us take a look at what the French police notes in their report:
"I, Felix Mangaud, police superintendent in the district Faubourg-du-Roule, continue my investigation and put the following items under seal. (Mangaud is the

officer that noted and should have taken care of cartridge number two in the sequence). Seal no. 1: One 9 mm automatic pistol, manufactured by Browning in Herstal in Belgium with no. 360,413 which had been used by Mr. Kreuger in connection with his suicide (with magazine).

Seal no. 2: one shell of 9 mm caliber, found beside the body, coming from the cartridge with which Mr. Kreuger shot himself.

Seal no. 3: one cartridge, which was found in the magazine of the pistol, at the moment it was found.

Seal no. 4: one shirt of yellow/white silk, marked with the letters IK, on which there was a hole, edges of which were ragged and blackened by burning powder and to a high degree drenched in blood—the shirt taken from Kreuger's body.

Seal no. 5: an under waistcoat of yellow/white silk marked with the letters IK on which on the left breast side was a small round hole which to a high degree was drenched in blood. The west has been taken from Mr. Kreuger's body.

Seal no. 6 a west of gray cloth, stained with blood, but not broken through by the bullet as Mr. Kreuger had unbuttoned it.

Police superintendent
Mangaud"

This report of registration was made March 13th 1932 and it is also this report that I found in the Riksarkiv when I studied it at the end of the 1980s. As you can see the second cartridge in the sequence is missing. Is it possible that the superintendent—the day after he got the case in his hands—simply forgot the second cartridge in the sequence while he is registering all the other items? He had emptied the weapon; noted in his report that the weapon was still loaded with two cartridges, one in the barrel and one in the magazine. And he had all the items in front of himself while working. Should he not have noticed if there was one cartridge left on the table after that? Did he not read his own notes? Was it such a poor job from the side of the police (such things have happened—even French Superintendents are humans). Or—was there simply no second cartridge?

The Swedish police record from 1933 is of no higher caliber. The police investigator, switches between revolver and pistol and tries to correct the French report where he believes it to be wrong. In Sweden—at least today—there is a rule that a suicide should be looked upon as a crime, i.e. a murder until there is no doubt what so ever, that it is a suicide. This rule may not have existed in 1932, or was temporarily forgotten. Everyone seems to have accepted Miss Bokman's information: "My boss has committed suicide (or possibly shot himself)."

If we take another look at the police doctor's report we find that he came to Kreuger's apartment at around 4.00 p.m. and examined Kreuger's body which he maintains was found at 12 o'clock with a bullet from a revolver shot at the left side of his chest. We know that Kreuger was not found until roughly 13.30 and that he was not shot with a revolver. Dr. Grille further notes that it is difficult to follow the trace of the bullet entering the body. At the end of his examination Dr. Marcel Grille states: "The death seems to have been caused by suicide with a handgun. The bullet has wounded the artery and caused an immediate death."

The value of the whole investigation must be considered at the best to be questionable.

A question that frequently has been asked is if a bullet from a 9 mm gun does not penetrate the body. In other words should you not have found also an outgoing hole? The immediate reply is of course, yes. However, there are two other possibilities to be considered. The bullet could have hit bone and been diverted in the body and got stuck in the spine or somewhere else. The other possibility is that the ammunition in those days could have been of such a poor quality that the bullet did not get power enough to completely penetrate the body. We are supposed to be dealing with a 9 mm. bullet and a bullet hole from that type of a cartridge is said to have a characteristic look—a small round hole with blue/black edges (as we will see a little further on). No description of the hole has been given so we do not even know if it was a bullet wound.

Many times I have been asked the question why someone should try to put the gun in Kreuger's left hand? Why not the right—it should be more natural. Of course it should—but Kreuger was on his back to the left in a double bed. The left hand was the closest. However, it is not impossible that an attempt was made to put the gun in his right hand but without success and that is when the waistcoat got its blood stains. Another explanation could be that the one who fired the shot was in a hurry. Maybe his mission was to arrange a suicide that could stand for a first inspection, and that he was assured that there would not be a more thorough investigation.

As all experts today declare that Kreuger most probably could not have shot himself with either the right or the left hand, there are not so many alternatives left. I can only think of one, and that is an inverted grip where you would pull the trigger with one of the thumbs. With this grip however and under the given conditions you could not fill the other criteria. Therefore this possibility has been discarded.

Everything put together indicates that Ivar Kreuger most probably did not shoot himself, and if he did not shoot himself, somebody else did and if somebody else shot him—he was murdered.

If you have followed the case and my reasoning so far you might say that an autopsy would clearly show, if Kreuger had held the gun and if so in which hand. It would have given us the caliber of the bullet and we would have known if Kreuger had been drugged and a dozen other things. If you are thinking along those lines you are doing a bit of correct thinking. The French authorities offered to do an autopsy in Paris but the Swedish Minister Ehrensvärd said that he did not think that it was necessary, and if it was, it would be done in Sweden. We should remember that the French police doctor recommended an autopsy and the Kreuger family also asked that one should be carried out. Everything was prepared for an autopsy in **Stockholm** when it suddenly was inhibited by the Governor of Stockholm, Nils Edén (according to information, after a visit from important people).

Inhibited?! Forbidden?! It is criminal. That is the reaction I get from police investigators and doctors of forensic medicine today.

New Ideas, Information, Investigations And Answers

You could say that what I have written above is more or less a summary of my first book on the subject. During the spring of 1999 I held three lectures about Ivar Kreuger and to my joy a surprising majority of the more than 600 listener came to share my opinion that Kreuger had been killed.

When the book had been published I felt that I had done my part. I felt that I had shown that Kreuger did not commit suicide and that the road was open for a new and impartial investigation. I wanted to drop the case. But it was easier said than done. I could not let got. There were some questions that had not received a 100% satisfactory answer. Why did the man who bought the gun want the cartridges separated from the gun? How come that the second cartridge in the sequence possibly had been missing? Why could not the doctor follow the trace of the bullet entering the body? How did Ivar Kreuger come to rest, fully dressed, on his bed?

In my first book, published in Sweden, I had touched on the possibility that Kreuger could have been drugged. I had dropped that thought because it required some inside help. Based upon the research material I had at the time, I was unable to prove anything further. The original purpose had been just that—to show that Kreuger had been murdered. However, sometimes your subconscious mind keeps working, on its own. In old detective stories it was very often the butler that had something to do with the crime—either alone or in the form of helping someone else. Kreuger did not have a butler—but a housekeeper—Jeanette Barrault. It might be worthwhile to check her out once more.

Barrault was also the name of the banker that worked together with the former Counselor of Legation, Sabatier d'Espeyran, who later was prosecuted together with several other persons and sentenced for several crimes against Kreuger (forged certificates of deposit; the sale of contracted collateral etc.). Hardly anything was mentioned about this matter in the Swedish press. A suspicious claim has been made that the two Barraults were related. I have not been able, so far, to track this information, or its basis.

We know that Miss Barrault served Kreuger breakfast roughly 8.30 a.m. on Saturday March 12th. At 10.45 he declared that he got suddenly very tired. This information was given by Miss Bokman. Miss Barrault goes shopping 10.45 and returns 12.10 (her own information, given in connection with a police hearing). According to research made by the French journalist Georges Arque, this was not Miss Barrault's ordinary shopping time. To shop one hour and twenty five minutes for food for lunch seems to be a long time. Especially, as Kreuger had a meeting and could be expected to have lunch with the members of the meeting.

Let us have a look at the records of the police hearing. This is what she said:

"There are no doubts about that Mr. Kreuger has taken his own life."

How on earth could she know anything about this, and who asked for her opinion?

"I do not hesitate for a moment saying that Mr. Kreuger bought the gun the previous day."

The hearing was held Sunday March 13th. Exactly what she means with "previous day" is unknown. It could have meant Saturday. However, she told the police that Kreuger was alone in the apartment when she was out shopping. How could she possibly know that? If she meant Friday then we know that Kreuger could not have bought the gun as we can account for every moment of the day. But whatever day she meant is not the important thing in this case. The important thing is that Miss Barrault knows that the gun has been bought. The police did not know that until Monday. Who had told Miss Barrault about the purchase of the gun?

Going over the case once more—we know, that the days after the 12th. there was a lot of activity in Kreuger's apartment. Stacking documents, packing documents, burning documents and probably also removing documents. All possible places and rooms were searched. Just the same, Miss Barrault finds the 97 remaining cartridges in a wardrobe! Someone else ought to have found them first—that is if they had been there at the time.

According to criminal investigators that I have discussed the case with, it is not uncommon that someone who is not a direct suspect talks too much. They talk much and initiate matters that they have not been asked about and things they should not know about. They fuss around trying to assist with the investigation. Similar to what Miss Barrault does in this case. You should listen to these people. Sooner or later they might just talk a little too much. But that requires of course an investigation, an interrogator and a possible prosecutor. Such things did not exist in the Kreuger case.

Miss Barrault informed the police that she looked through the keyhole and/or that she opened the door to Kreuger's bedroom just a little bit and saw that Kreuger was asleep. There have been no reasons to question this. In fact at a first glance it appears logical. Let us do exactly what she has said that she was doing. Look at the sketch of Kreuger's apartment and let us in our mind walk up to the bedroom door, which at that moment of course was closed. Let us bend over and look through the keyhole. It is impossible to see Kreuger's bed from that position. And remember, Kreuger was on the left side of the double bed, in other words, as far from the keyhole view as possible. The case will be the same if you open the door just a little crack. You will not be able to see the bed.

Conclusion: Miss Barrault is telling a lot of lies. Why?

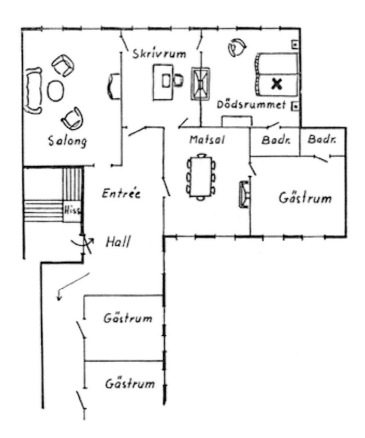

Kreugers apartment: Gästrum = guest room; Skrivrum = study; Matsal = dining room; Dödsrummet = Ivar Kreugers bed room.

Could it be that she was the one that left the door open so that the murderer could enter the apartment? Could she have slipped some medical drug into Kreuger's breakfast that would affect him a few hours later?

When the phone rings Miss Barrault says that she went to look for Kreuger. Possibly she did not do that at all—she knew that Kreuger was either asleep from the drug she had given him or that he was already dead. Maybe she should be taken on her words *".and can not be disturbed."*

Possibly Miss Barrault had been informed about the purchase of the gun and been instructed to stay away from the apartment between 10.45 a.m. and 12.10 p.m.

Thinking along these lines, I came to think of the possibility that Kreuger had not been shot at all. He could very well have been murdered with a stiletto like instrument and in order to arrange a suicide a blank shot was fired to cover the wound. This would answer the question why the doctor could not follow the trace of the bullet entering the body; why there was no exit hole; why there had been a considerable bloodshed. It could also mean that Kreuger had been killed somewhere else in the apartment and then had been carried to the bed where the arrangements with the gun were made.

Just for the moment I do not have a good answer to the question why a possible murderer did not shoot Kreuger directly other than special circumstances in connection with the killing and the arrangement of the "suicide".

A killing with a stiletto like instrument is quiet, effective, and should not create great bloodshed. Kreuger's body evidenced great blood shed, as seen on the body's back . . . This could have arisen when the body was moved from the place of killing to the bed. To cover the hole from the stiletto with a blank shot is quite logical, as it would be difficult to maintain a suicide with a stiletto. A blank shot would give the necessary characteristic powder burns from a contact shot and would be sufficient for a quick investigation. A closer investigation would of course show that there were now traces of particles from the powder burns on the inside of the textile garments. The more you think of it, the more probable this line of thinking appears.

A Letter That Gets Another Meaning

In response to an article that I wrote in the magazine *The Swedish Market,* a relative to the Swedish Consul in Paris 1932, Mr. L G Forrsius, informed me that Forrsius had stated that he had seen Kreuger's dead body on the bed. Forrsius said that you could see traces of the muzzle that in some way had been moving over the shirt around the bullet hole. If this information is correct—which I do not doubt—there can be several reasons for this. But right now it fits the picture quite well. If you already have a whole in the shirt after the stiletto and want to cover this hole with a shot it is of course difficult to get the muzzle over the hole right off. You probably would have to try several times before getting a reasonable fit. If that should be the case there is no wonder that the muzzle has been moved back and forth in order to get full coverage.

An Interesting Point Of Timing

When my first book was published I got a great number of letters and phone calls from people in Sweden but also from some other countries. I must say that all of them were very kind and positive. One letter, from the editor, Ake Sandstrom, also contained an article, which was of such interest that I am taking the liberty to make a summary of its contents.

In March 1932 Mr. Sandstrom lived in Berlin where he studied. At the same boarding house as Sandstrom lived a Mr. Gabriel Safarana, Secretary at the Turkish Legation. March 12th at 12.45 (give or take five minutes) Safarana came rushing into Mr. Sandstrom's room and said that through the Legation he had been informed that Kreuger had committed suicide in Paris. This information is of course extremely interesting. The information of Kreuger's death should have reached the Turkish Legation in Berlin prior to the time that Kreuger's body was discovered in Paris, by Littorin and Bokman. And in any case prior to the time when the discovery was reported officially. How long time could it have taken for this information to reach Berlin? A more detailed description can be read in *Sydsvenska Dagbladet* dated March 12th 1967.

I believe that this piece of news would be well worth some further research—if it is not too late.

During the time I researched and worked on my first book I did not want to get in touch with the Kreuger family in order not to be influenced by the subjective opinions that might have existed about the available material. A few years after the book's publication, I met a few family members. At that meeting a few very important questions, were brought up that I believe require more research.

The most important came from Eva Dyrssen the daughter of one of Ivar Kreuger's sisters. She was present when Doctor Karlmark, who was going to perform the autopsy of Kreuger, checked the body the day prior to the autopsy. She had and still has a clear memory of what happened at that occasion. When I heard what she had to tell, I asked her to get in touch with the press as my name had no weight. I will return to this matter later.

The other information was also a bit extraordinary. A German lawyer had informed the family, that Ivar Kreuger still was registered—at least as late as in 1997—as the legal owner of some major pieces of property in the center of Berlin. The case is very complicated as the estate of Ivar Kreuger was declared in bankruptcy. The case has been dismissed for many years and there are no legal representatives available. The case also calls for a united family, but the family is split and live all over the globe.

Why I took an interest in this part was because I recalled an instruction, given by the administrators of Kreuger & Toll to the international accounting firm that was called in. The instructions were that the accounting firm was not to bother with the interests in Deutsche Union Bank, neither with the real estate in Berlin or Paris. Deutsche Union Bank, a majority holding, was evaluated by Jacob Wallenberg (Stockholms Enskilda Bank) to 0 (Zero). The real estate in question was not accounted for.

It is not difficult to come to the conclusion—without a long row of figures—that if this was the way Kreuger & Toll's and Ivar Kreuger's assets were treated (and it was), it is no surprise that Kreuger's opponents managed to have both estates declared in bankruptcy. Furthermore, the case with the German real estate shows that the managers simply could not care less. They were legal people with no knowledge of business what so ever.

TV-series about Ivar Krueger

(pure fiction)

In 1998 Swedish TV showed a series about Ivar Kreuger. It was pure fiction but was never the less liked by the public, and awoke a new interest in Kreuger. I was contacted by various journalists and told them to call Eva Dyrssen to find out what she remembered from March 1932.

In certain newspapers you could on the 30th December 1998, under the headline:

"Murder, said the doctor!"

read, that Eva Dyrssen, the niece of Ivar Kreuger, at that time 22 years old, was present when Dr. Karlmark checked the body before the planned autopsy and that she never forgot what the doctor said:

"This is not a suicide. It is a well planned murder."

I want to underline the fact that this statement (based on seeing and hearing) was made by a today living witness. Other persons, authors, historians and whatever they claim to be, can say whatever they want. It is furthermore important to note that Dr. Karlmark is, as far as we know, the only expert that has been able to give a statement in this particular case, based on an inspection.

Eva Dyrssen's statements have been video taped, and preserved for future research.

As mentioned earlier, the autopsy was inhibited, after Karlmark's inspection, by the Governor of Stockholm, Nils Edén. Prior to the inhibition, a few prominent people had been visiting Mr. Edén.

Inhibition of the Autopsy

What do we know about Nils Edén

We know from letters by the Chief of the County Secretariat A. Beckius and by the former Court-Martial Prosecutor C. Malm, that Mr. Edén in March of 1932 was visited by some prominent persons who urged him to inhibit the autopsy of Ivar Kreuger. We also know that the autopsy was promptly inhibited, and that all documents, in the case thereafter, were destroyed by Mr. Edén. We know further that the autopsy should have been carried out early in the morning of March 22nd and that unknown, prominent people visited Mr. Edén late in the afternoon/early evening on March 21st. Therefore, we can pin-point the visit in time to be shortly after doctor Karlmark's words **"This is not a suicide. It is a well planned murder"**.

Nils Edén had probably no personal interest in whether an autopsy was carried out on Kreuger or not. Edén's knowledge in economics was practically non-existent, as was his knowledge of languages. A possible exception was German where he in an emergency could make himself understood (source: Marcus Wallenberg). Even if Edén, contrary to all expectations, should have had a negative opinion of Ivar Kreuger and his business, this should hardly have been a reason for Edén to inhibit the autopsy. One can also be quite sure that Edén did not have any knowledge what so ever of the importance of the autopsy in this particular case.

"Prominent persons"—that could have been any persons above a certain level in society. However, in this case, I believe that the number of persons can be reduced, if you follow certain criteria.

- They must be well known to Edén as he otherwise would not have received them at such short notice.
- They must be able to argue, persuade and underline the necessity of haste.
- They must be persons with strong economical, possibly also political, interests in the Kreuger affair.
- They must be persons with means to get Edén to do what they were asking him to do.
- They must be of Swedish nationality.

107

- Finally, they must be persons who knew why the autopsy of Ivar Kreuger, at any price, had to be inhibited. Otherwise the murder would be disclosed.

Exactly how the persuasion was made, what was said, what arguments were used, or whatever promises were given—we do not know. Edén might have made a note of it—or not.

I believe that the above criteria are important, as well as correct. Not just anybody, will approach the Governor of Stockholm, and ask for an emergency act to be carried through in a rather complex and delicate situation as this one.

I made a list of possible people and have been able to reduce the number to five plausible persons. However, of these five, two or possibly three could be removed with the same end result. The persons on my list are:

Marcus Wallenberg, Sr. (Stockholms Enskilda Bank). M. Wallenberg knew Edén very well. They had been traveling together on an official mission to England and they had exchanged letters, in political questions, during a number of years.

Johannes Hellner (Board Member of Stockholms Enskilda Bank). When Edén formed the first parliamentary government with liberals and social democrats, Johannes Hellner was elected Foreign Minister. Hellner is said to have been a very nice man who always did whatever Marcus Wallenberg told him to do.

Eliel Löfgren was elected, Minister of Justice in Edén's government and later became leader of the liberal party. Löfgren was a lawyer, and as legal adviser, he and Hellner were going to play an important part in connection with the administration of the two Kreuger estates.

Hugo Stenbeck. I do not know if Mr. Stenbeck knew Edén. However, that in itself does not make any difference, as a phone call from Marcus Wallenberg would open the door for him. Stenbeck could get almost any matter settled here and now, and that would be his roll in the negotiations with Edén.

Fredrik von Dardel. This could be the fifth name. His position at Karolinska Sjukhuset (hospital), where the autopsy should have taken place and at the Ministry of Health could have been important. Later we will take a closer look at von Dardel and his connections with Marcus Wallenberg.

I think that a combination of two or three of the above mentioned persons could probably persuade Edén to inhibit the autopsy. My bet would be:

Johannes Hellner as a representative for Stockholms Enskilda Bank, referring to Marcus Wallenberg and Eliel Löfgren.

Hugo Stenbeck as a representative of the "Royal Commission" (that did not exist). He would be the one that organized the whole thing to take place here and now. Stenbeck would be the most likely person to advise Edén to destroy all documents in the case.

Dardel, representing the Ministry of Health, and as expert of medical matters in general.

I do not think that Marcus Wallenberg would show up in a situation like this—he did not want to be seen. Neither do I think that Eliel Löfgren at this time knew all the details of the case. It might be worth noting that all the above mentioned persons had a legal background.

We also know that Mr. Nils Edén was born on the 25th of August 1871 in the town of Piteå in the northern part of Sweden and he died in Stockholm on June 6th 1945. He spent most of his active life in politics. In 1920 he was elected Governor of Stockholm a position that he held until 1938. He left politics in 1923 and began to write. When he was working on the second part of his memoirs (which would cover the period of 1932) a fire started, for unknown reasons, in his library, in Edén's 12—room apartment, at Odengatan 2 in Stockholm, on the night to the 19th November 1944. Edén got severely burned and died in June the following year. His widow donated all his notes and papers to the Library of the University of Uppsala where the file marked "Memories" is marked with *SPÄRR* meaning blocked.

Expertise on Forensic Medicine 1999

To my thinking and theories, I could now add the information from Eva Dyrssen about Dr. Karlmark's statement in connection with the planned autopsy. This would be the right time to consult experts on forensic medicine in order to see if some additional information could be obtained. I got in touch with the assistant chief physician Olle Lindquist at the Institution of Forensic Medicine in Uppsala and on January 26th 1999. As earlier mentioned Dr. Lindquist is, among other things, an expert on murder and suicide with handguns.

I did not mention anything about my own ideas. Unbiased we went through all the material that I had available in the form of police records, the reports from the police doctor and the inhibition of the autopsy.

Dr. Lindquist wanted to question the possibility of a contact shot. He pointed out the lack of powder burns on the inside of the garments. Observed the "round hole" in the under waist coat and that this had been left without any comments regarding damage or burns. We discussed the French doctor's difficulty to follow the bullet's entrance into the body and touched the possibility of a wound caused by a stab or thrust.

Suddenly I could hear Dr Lindquist say more or less to himself: "It is really enough to shoot just powder".

I thought that this was just the right time to ask one—for me crucial question—"What can Dr Karlmark have seen in order for him—at a quick glance—to judge that it was not a case of suicide but a well planned murder?"

Dr. Lindquist thought for a moment before saying: "The entrance hole—he probably saw that it was not a bullet hole."

Dr Lindquist continued after a little while: "Kreuger could have been drugged and killed with a stiletto like instrument—like a knitting needle with a ring in the end. This is an instrument that have been used a number of times by agents during the war. The ring makes it easy to pull out. Then you shoot a blank that is a cartridge where the bullet itself has been replaced with wax or for instance some grease. This will, at a quick glance, cover the hole from a stab as the first layer of garments will get the characteristic powder and soot marks. A killer is not interested in producing two entrance holes, which you will get if you have a fully loaded cartridge in the covering shot."

We continued our discussion around what he just had said, and when I was about to leave Dr. Lindquist said: "The people, who arranged with the inhibition of the autopsy, against the advise from the French doctor, against the advise from two of Sweden's top experts on forensic medicine, and against the request from the family, must have had a very important reason for getting the autopsy inhibited. Otherwise you do not behave in that way".

This is the reaction from experts on forensic medicine today.

An autopsy could have given us the answer also for those questions required for confirming a possible suicide. But apparently an autopsy had to be stopped.

The theory of how Kreuger was killed had now received support. But why was he not shot directly? Was it possibly because it would be more difficult to arrange the "appearance" of suicide—or because a blank cartridge would make less noise?

In order to get an answer to these questions, I got in touch with a Criminal Investigator who was very familiar with the type of gun, a Browning 9 mm. that was used in 1932. He did not know much about the Kreuger case, but got very upset when he heard that the autopsy had been inhibited. However, he did not believe that there was too big a difference between the sounds from a blank, or a fully loaded cartridge. But he gave me some interesting information. If you use a blank the power of the powder gases would probably not be great enough to reload the gun. In order to get the empty shell out you would have to work the mechanism manually. In doing so you would get cartridge No. 2 in the sequence in your hand and either take care of it or put it into the chambre.

Could this be the answer to the question about where the No. 2 cartridge had gone, and why it was not registered by the police?

I could now add more and more answers to previously open questions.

Was it possible that the man who bought the gun separated the cartridges from the gun in order to have some of them prepared as blanks?

Was it possible that there were two blanks made just in case something would go wrong?

When only one blank was used the other one would have to be removed one way or the other and that is why, it was not registered by the police.

The round hole in the under waist coat with only bloodstains was probably from a stiletto like instrument.

The unclear entrance hole, that the French doctor noted, was probably caused by a stiletto like instrument.

The position of the gun in Kreuger's left hand was probably caused by haste. The "cramped grip", described by Littorin, was caused when the gun was forced into Kreuger's hand where one of the fingers was stiff and could not be used in the grip.

Kreuger could have put himself on the bed when he was overwhelmed of tiredness in order to take a quick nap before the meeting and he himself unbuttoned his coat and waistcoat. Alternatively he could have gone to sleep in an easy chair, got stabbed and was carried to the bed. This alternative could explain how the waistcoat got bloodstains and the unmotivated amounts of blood to Kreuger's back.

The autopsy was inhibited because, what is said above, or similar theories were too close to the truth—that is—what really happened.

—

Dr. Erik Karlmarks Notes

When I was about to finish this book I came across an interesting document labelled "The experience of a doctor of forensic medicine from the days after the death of Ivar Kreuger". I decided to make a few extracts in order to support previously received information.

Dr. Karlmark writes:

"Many of the circumstances around the death are obscure, some less obscure, but as much could be said that a police investigation in connection with such a death should have been carried out with a much higher degree of severity in Sweden in 1932 compared with what was done in France the same year.

—

It is difficult to get a clear and exact picture from the police report of the situation in which Kreuger was found and it is not known if the police authorities had any photographs taken at the place, nor if they had tried to arrange with any form of reconstruction—a task that would not have required any great costs or hard work.

—

I have not previously put anything of what follows in writing. Possibly can these notes be of some interest in the future.

—

When it became known that Krueger had died and that his body was going to be transported to Stockholm and the matter handled in the administrative district of Stockholm, the police superintendent William Bergenfelt, a personal friend of mine, consulted with Axel Thour, who later became the chief of the Statepolice Criminal Dept. Bergenfelt, used, as I well know, in matters that involved great responsibility consult this experienced criminal investigator. They expressed as their opinion that an autopsy of Kreugers body was necessary. Bergenfelt informed the chief of the District Office, district secretary Beckius, probably as a reply to his question. Bergenfelt as well as Thour have personally informed me about this.

113

Jonas Angstrom

—

At the time of Krueger's death, Professor Gunnar Hedrén was head of the Dept. of Forensic Medicinie at Karolinska Institutet and the author of these notes was assistant surgeon. Hedrén called the attention to the importance of an autopsy and Beckius was informed of Hedéns opinion. Beckius as well as District Assessor Malm had sent written memoranda to the Governor of Stockholm with more or less the same contents i.e. that an autopsy was necessary. Thus the need of an autopsy was the opinion of the countrys foremost experts in forensic medicine, Hedrén, of the District of Stockholms two legal experts Beckius and Malm, of the Districts Police Superintendent together with a very experienced criminologist, Thour.

—

With the very strict and many times to the point juridical correctness which was characteristic for Hedréns way to administrate his office, I consider it impossible that he should have given instructions to prepare for an autopsy without having received information to do so from the Governors Office. Hedrén got very upset as he realised that a great amount of material and evidence would be lost for ever from further investigations. Everybody working at the institution for forensic medicine was utterly stunned over the Governors decision although we at that time did not know that Beckius as well as Malm in special written memoranda had stressed the necessity that an autopsy should be performed.

—

My experience from Governor Edéns way to handle autopsy cases in connection with forensic medicine had shown me that Edén was a careful man who was not inclined to overlook anything. In the newspapers it can be read that I about 15 years ago expressed my respect for Edéns actions in such cases. What it was that lead to that this careful and experienced man made such a decision in a case so full of investigation errors and contradictory information and against the united expertice point of view has during 17 years been and still is a riddle to me."
(1453-1455)

—

**With the presentation of all these facts the myth of Ivar Kreuger's suicide
can now be declared to be a lie.**

Ivar Kreuger's opponents were very good at creating myths and this is a good place to get rid of another one.

114

The Myth of the farewell letters

Many times I have been surprised at how people have paid so much attention to what has been called the *"farewell letters"* which means the three letters that were found in the apartment after Kreuger's death. I have seen copies and read two of them. The third, which does not exist any longer, was written to Kreuger's sister, Britta, but I have a fair idea of what it contained. Of the two other letters one was to Sheele/Alsing and the other to Krister Littorin. Only the letter to Littorin was dated March 12th 1932. In none of the letters were there even the slightest sign of the intention of committing suicide. Neither is the writer expressing any signs of being unbalanced or depressed. Thus there are no reasons what so ever to have named the letters "farewell letters".

The letter to Littorin is by hand, written in English and as follows:

"12th March 1932
Dear Krister,
    I have made such a mess of things that I believe this to be the most satisfactory solution for everybody concerned. Please take care of these two letters and also see that two letters which were sent a couple of days ago by Jordahl to me at 5 Avenue Victor Emanuel are returned to Jordahl. The letters were sent by Majestic. Goodbye now and thanks.
                                                                                                        I.K

It should be observed that this letter was not shown to the public until roughly 23 years later.

This however, was nothing that those who managed the whole case, including the mass media, could accept. I am not going to quote all that was written but only those parts that I feel are of immediate interest. Things that are completely wrong I will print in italics; lies or distorted information that is disinformation will be in italics underlined. My own comments will be in brackets. Those who would be interested in the complete content of the articles can find them in the Royal Library where all newspapers have been microfilmed.

Svenska Dagbladet 13th March 1932
    "To day at noon Mr. Ivar Kreuger took his own life by a shot from a *revolver* in the heart. He committed this deed of desperation in his home, Avenue Victor Emanuel III, 5."

"Mr. Kreuger arrived here yesterday from New York, and *in the evening he dined together with some other Swedes, who participate in the conference of the International Chamber of Commerce.* No one noticed anything special with Kreuger."

"He had arranged to meet around noon with American, English and French bankers. Kreuger did not turn up at the meeting and they began to be worried about him. Mr. Littorin, who also was a member of the conference, went to Kreuger's apartment. In the bedroom he found Kreuger fully dressed on the bed seemingly without life. *The doctor that had been summoned, established that he had shot himself with a bullet through the heart with a revolver.*"

"Kreuger was tired of life. Depressed already in the morning. Breakdown. Suffered from heart disease with feelings of agony." (Headlines).

Littorin is supposed to have said: "He was dressed in a dark suit and held an automatic pistol in a cramped grip. On the table there were three letters. One had my address."

"In this letter Kreuger declared that he was tired of life and business and wanted an end to it all. He asked for forgiveness. Thereafter follows some calm, clear instructions of pure business characteristics.

I can find no other explanation to Kreuger's suicide than a mental collapse.

The New York doctors had urged him to be extremely careful on account of his heart disease that all the time gave him strong feelings of agony. It was possibly these feelings of agony that finally caused him to take this desperate step."

(Now, where can you find any of the above in the letter written by Kreuger to Littorin? A few days later the press changed "heart disease" to "brain fatigue". As long as it was about sickness the press did not seem to care and the whole thing was really sick).

"Here in Paris some of his collaborators have gathered. Bank director Rydbeck arrived a few days ago. According to information there were no exceptional matters in the Kreuger Group that needed immediate attention right now".

(I have found an interesting interview with Miss Barrault)

"As she got the opinion that he had gone back to sleep again she went out and returned first after a little while to report that breakfast was served. That is when she found Mr. Kreuger dead on the settee with a revolver on the floor beside him. Almost at the same moment Mr. Littorin

arrived and got naturally very upset over what had happened and informed immediately the Police Superintendent in the district".

(Observe that the automatic pistol now has become a revolver that has fallen down on the floor. Nothing is correct.).

"*On a table beside the bed* there were three letters, one addressed to one of Ivar Kreuger's four sisters, one to Littorin and to a personal friend in Stockholm. *In the letter to Littorin Kreuger explains the conditions that had driven him to this desperate action and describes the financial difficulties he had had during the last months".*

(Where in Kreuger's Letter to Littorin can you read this? One should also keep in mind that Kreuger and Littorin were in daily contact either by phone or telegram.).

In Dagens Nyheter you could read:

"Farewell letter to his friend*: "I am exhausted and can not go on any longer . . ."*

"The Letter to Littorin is written in English, *and Kreuger writes that his doctors in America have urgently declared to him that in order to save his nerves he will have to withdraw completely from business. He continues to tell that he is completely exhausted and no longer in a condition to handle the difficulties that the crisis had brought.*

(Dagens Nyheter has, apart from the above, the same description as Svenska Dagbladet. Above quotes are from 13th of March 1932. End of quotes).

At a time when a large part of the Swedish people (savers and shareholders) is hit by something that could be described as a traumatic chock the big daily newspapers choose to engage in a pure disinformation campaign spreading the news of Ivar Kreuger's suicide. Based on what facts? Based only upon Miss Bokman's opinion when she reports to the police and the police' acceptance of her judgement. In other words, based on no facts at all. As the press can not get facts it creates *facts* of its own, out of thin air, in order to indoctrinate its readers. This is the way that general and contemporary opinion was created so that everybody in the future should know and be able to tell that Ivar Kreuger committed suicide. This was probably organized manipulation of the media so that nobody should dare to raise the question, if Kreuger really committed suicide or was murdered. Neither raises any questions about what happened afterwards.

But one must ask the question: "How can disinformation of this kind be created and then spread to the people of Sweden (Sweden in this case, other countries in other cases.) And who was behind this? It might not be difficult to understand why it was created, as the aim was to create a time of instability and possibly also of panic, in order to make a take over possible without any major opposition.

I will try to give an answer to the questions and explain the situation.

When the death of Ivar Kreuger was made known in Sweden, late in the afternoon of the 12th of March, the decision was made not to make it official until after the close of the European Stock Exchanges. When the news was finally released, the newspapers had to have something to write. But what? Therefore, the following cable was sent by Dagens Nyheter to their representative in Paris:

"Herr Nils Widstrand
46 RUEBOLOGNY PARIS 17
INTERVJUA GENERALKONSUL SACHS SOM ÄR I PARIS
DAGENS NYHETER"

(Interview consul general Sachs who is in Paris)
(This cable was sent March 12th 1932 at 19.40 with the serial no. 021714. The original can be found in Uppsala).

Who was Consul Sachs? About Josef Sachs we know the following. He was a member of the Board of Stockholms Enskilda Bank. In the morning of March 12th he had called Mr. Jacob Wallenberg, who was in London, in order to inform him that he, Josef Sachs[9], had a feeling that something was going to happen just this particular day, and he recommended Wallenberg to return to Stockholm. Wallenberg is supposed to have replied that he also had a feeling that something was going to happen, and had therefore already booked his return ticket to Sweden.

Not only do we here find two persons—that irrespectively of each other—has a strange feeling that requires at least one of them to immediately return to Stockholm. How realistic is this?

Secondly, we find that Mr. Josef Sachs and the persons, with whom he worked, are those who supplied the Swedish journalists in Paris and through them the Swedish people, with the lies and the information that Ivar Kreuger had committed suicide. And we should keep in mind that this has not been proved or disproved ever since.

[9]   From Joseph Sach´s memoirs

Let Us For A Moment Do A Bit Of Conspiracy Thinking

Generally I do not like this, but sometimes it is necessary and can give new angles.

Ivar Kreuger was murdered and the murder was well planned (*Dr. Karlmark and others*).

Some of those who knew of the plans, alternatively were part of the planning group, had been informed about the approximate time, when the murder was to take place. They were now prepared to spread disinformation and if possible, create a panic (*Josef Sachs' own information, pages 107-109 in my first book*).

It was planned that a *revolver* was going to be bought and that a suicide was going to be arranged by a bullet through the heart.

A farewell letter was included in the planning. It was intended to be logical, in its content, in such a way that there would be no questions about, whether or not, there were suicide intentions behind it. The general content of the letter was to be known, ahead of time, by those who were going to spread the "news" and disinformation.

Everything was prepared.

But everything went wrong already from the beginning. Possibly on account of nervousness and haste because it was made known (*by Schéle*) that Kreuger was prepared to disclose his opponent's wrong doings and that he had returned from America with complete and compromising evidence.

The man who bought the gun made the first mistake. He began to hesitate between a revolver and a pistol and ended up buying a pistol. *This information was not passed on.*

The murder was done according to plan—with a stiletto. To cover the wound with a blank from a revolver should have been comparatively easy. The empty shell remains in the magazine. If you, just in case, should have needed two blanks, it would have been quite easy to change the remaining blank against one fully loaded.

119

When the covering shot was fired with the pistol, the coverage as such functioned as it should, but it was then, that the problems arose. When the empty shell, that the pistol should eject, was not ejected on account of too low power from the powder gases, the murderer had to take out the shell manually. But before he could get at the empty shell, cartridge No. 2 had come forward from the magazine. It might have been another blank, or a fully loaded—it does not matter for our reasoning. The empty shell is taken out of the chambre and placed on the floor. The pistol is "closed". Everything looks normal—apart from one thing. The cartridge No. 2 should be in the chamber and not in the pocket of the murderer (if that is where it went). Possibly, this incident could be accounted for by the fact that the murderer was not fully accustomed with the gun in question (*according to the gun dealer*). It is also possible that the No. 2 cartridge is put into the chamber manually. The killer tries now to put the gun into Kreuger's right hand, but finds it rather difficult, as he more or less would have to climb the bed in doing so. The left hand is closer and will do, even if the stiff finger gives the grip a sort of cramped look.

According to plans, the farewell letter was to be placed in a suitable location. However, the killer finds—possibly to his relief—that there already was a letter that with enough cover and secrecy would do as a farewell letter. There were of course a lot of other documents stuck to it, but they could be separated, without any difficulties. Maybe it was better after all with one of Kreuger handwritten letters even if it was a bit unclear, than with a farewell letter that was forged. The completely forged letter was not used. *This information was not passed on.*

The discovery of Ivar Kreuger's death and the investigation by the police (if you want to call it by such a name), as above.

When Sweden was officially informed about the death of Ivar Kreuger, Bonnier (owner of Dagens Nyheter and a member of the Board of Stockholms Enskilda Bank), asked Dagens Nyheter, to interview Josef Sachs (also he a member of the Board of Stockholms Enskilda Bank), who was in Paris at the time. At the moment when Sachs was interviewed, the letter found in Kreuger's apartment had been taken care of, which made it impossible for Sachs or anybody else to discuss its contents. However, for Sachs this made no difference, as he roughly knew its contents.

At least that is what he thought.

He was telling the journalists, far and wide, about the revolver with which Kreuger shot himself through the heart and, about Kreuger's explanation for the suicide in the farewell letter—and of course, gets everything wrong.

Apparently it is Josef Sachs that is responsible for the disinformation "suicide with a revolver" that is hammered into the minds of the Swedish people, and so thoroughly that journalists and historians still are convinced that Josef Sachs' stories are in accordance with the truth.

Is this really the way it was? Those who support the theory of suicide will naturally look upon my speculation as a pure product of fantasy. True, but what is the alternative? That Sachs and all the journalists were myth maniacs? If so, Sachs might have infected quite a lot of people in his surroundings.

Josef Sachs wrote his memoir "The Saldo/Sum of my Life". In this he describes how he and Jacob Wallenberg, at the same day get the same feeling. One in Paris and the other one in London (see above). Sachs confirms this—in writing.

Sachs also describes a conversation with the Commercial Secretary Sven Bergius at the Swedish Legation:
      Bergius calls Sachs: "Have you heard anything about Kreuger today?—No. I have not. People are completely crazy. It is said that he has shot himself."

—   That is not impossible, I replied calmly.
—   What do you say? He cried out, terrified.
—   I said that I do not consider it impossible."

When Sachs gets back to Stockholm he was asked if he thought there were any wrong doings behind what had happened and he replied:

"It is difficult to say but there is always a possibility, considering that he took his own life".

I do not think that Josef Sachs statements are worth a deep analysis. I am satisfied with calling them remarkable.

In summing up the questions around the "farewell letter" there are a few points that I want to make before leaving it to the readers to decide what Kreuger's letter to Littorin concerned:

•   This is the only letter of the three that was dated March 12th.
•   The other two letters were dated in February 1932, both written in English.
•   The ending phrase is the same in this letter, as in one written to his friend Jordahl in a strictly business letter dated January/February.

Kreuger had spent much time teaching his collaborators that it is better to spend one or two additional words in a telegram to make the contents clear. He used to say: "We do not have the time to play with riddles." In his last letter however, he is supposed to have written: "I believe this to be the most satisfactory solution . . .". What "this"? There is no mentioning or sign what so ever of a suicide. Ivar Kreuger knew very well, that if he disappeared with all his knowledge of investments, secret negotiations and deposits in various names and of various types, there would be nothing less than chaos. Therefore, the sentence is ambiguous and rather meaningless.

- Ivar Kreuger wrote his name in one word, the two periods after I and K in IK should actually not be there.*
- Only if the letter was used as a missive will it get any meaning. That is, if there were additional documents attached to the letter and to which the letter refers.
- One ought to keep in mind that Ivar Kreuger and Krister Littorin were long time friends. They had been working together for more than 30 years. Is this short note, all that you would expect from one who is about to take his life's most important and desperate step? Is this all you have to say to a person who has been your friend for more than one half of your own life?

* I have found that Ivar Kreuger sometimes did use I.K. as a signature but *only* when he countersigned a lot of pages—for instance in a contract. In a cable to Littorin from Ile de France Kreuger sign with his first name—Ivar—which you would have expected him to do also in this case.

"7/3-32 Krilittorin Stockholm
Suggest you come to paris on Friday but telephone me elysee 7080 before seing anyone else—Ivar"

(DSCN 9599)

You can keep on asking questions about the letter, but personally I think that the time now is ripe to completely scrap the myth of the farewell letter.

Criticism

I welcome criticism when it is based on facts because then I can learn something. If it, however, is based on lack of knowledge and/or aims to ridicule, it only falls back on the critics themselves.

In my first book I touched on the possibility that the "farewell letter" could have been forged. A bank director—let us call him LET (he is having a book published in English and I do not want to make it difficult for him so I will only use his initials. LET immediately declared a possible forgery as pure nonsense and a desperate act to defend the theory of a murder.

I am not so sure that it was an impossible idea. I am not saying that it was a forgery— just, that it could possibly have been one. Let us see what Josef Sachs had to say about forgeries.

"With bold steps I entered the building where they were arranging the exhibition. I was fortunate to find some loose papers and envelopes marked with "Exposition Internationale des Filatelists" or whatever the name was. We went back to Menton, where Marcus (Marcus Wallenberg sr.) and I together wrote a letter in French, in which we pretended to be the Board of the Exposition. We had been informed that the famous Swedish stamp collector was visiting the Riviera and we wished him welcome to the opening ceremony. Another one of the friends, who was trained imitator of hand writings, wrote the letter with a pointed French pen in order to produce a typical French touch. That he signed the letter, F. Durant, was very consistent. As we did not have any official invitation cards, we came up with the idea that the letter should be valid as admission ticket. When we had accomplished this forgery, we sent a chauffeur to Monaco with an order to have it fit with a proper stamp and mailed to the hotel in Menton where our stamp collector was staying".

Of course this was a "practical joke" and of course it is pure coincident that the name Durant was the name of one of the directors in Lee Higginson & Co. But it still was a forgery and Sachs is using just that name for it. In other words my mentioning of the possibility of a forgery might after all not have been such a far-flung idea.

I can just as well give you two other examples of LET's way of arguing. Extract from a newspaper from 1998:

"LET mentions only one of Angstrom's points: When Kreuger was found he was holding the pistol in a cramped grip in his left hand".

"Pure invention and nonsense, writes LET, witnesses have said that the pistol was on the bed, next to his leg and that his arms were loosely stretched along his sides. Kreuger must have held the pistol in his right hand and when the shot was fired, it was thrown away by the recoil and ended up on the bed to the left of the dead".

Just remember that Krister Littorin was a first hand witness. He was interviewed the 12th, as well as the 13th of March 1932 and again his statements were mentioned in the press in 1949.

LET writes: "One other rather curious thing that Angstrom is making a big issue of is that Ivar Kreuger ordered a number of suits from his tailor before he left Paris for New York which he should not have done if he was thinking of committing suicide".

This is an interesting statement from LET, which goes to show how little he knows. When you follow a case like the one with Ivar Kreuger it is important to look at it from all possible angles. The financial and technical sides are only two. You also have the psychological side. Since psychology has to do with behaviorism, one has to find a pattern, followed by the subject, which may be a combination of specific behavior, likes and dislikes, and many other things. Once established one adds to it and compares one set of data to another in order to find out what the person is really like "on the inside" It is a very complicated matter, since one needs a great volume of data to make sense of any part of it. In creating such a pattern for Kreuger, the ordering of suits comes as one of several details. Obviously, LET does not know anything about these things. However, the way LET argues is dangerous for some readers. What he does is to extract *one* piece out of a chain of facts and tries to be funny about it—in a serious subject. Of course, if LET was placed on the stand to testify, relative to his handling of this matter, he would flunk and truly expose his own inabilities.

My publisher, Mr J Gillberg, has informed me that LET approached him, invited him for a lunch, and tried to prevent him from publishing my first book and that he also should have made an attempt to stop Eva Dyrsen from quoting what Dr. Karlmark said in connection with the autopsy. We can here add the fact that LET's behavior here shows his lack of ability to find a way out of his own psychological dilemma.

Enough now about LET (origin SEB) and his supporters. He seems to lack of knowledge of the case and ought to study what the experts say (below).

An Investigation By Criminologists And Experts On Handguns

An investigation regarding the possible use of a 9 mm Browning Pistol in connection with the death of Ivar Kreuger has been carried out by Kriminalhauptmeister Heinz Westphal, Hamburg, Germany, who also received the opinion of Kriminaloberamtmann Johann Fischer. Mr. Fischer had been in charge of "Die Kriminalpolizeiliche Todesermittlung".

The investigation report reads:

"When the body was found, there was a pistol, type FN-9 mm, in his left hand. One therefore came to the conslusion that he (Ivar Kreuger) had shot himself in the heart with his left hand. On account of my experience, I consider this to have been impossible. Why? Here are the particulars of the weapon in question (see photograph):

FABRIQUE NATIONALE D'ARMES DE GUERRE; HERSTAL, BELGIQUE BROWNING PATENT DEPOSE
Model 10/22 FN—Caliber 9 mm. Weight empty 685 g. With full magazine 762 g.
Pistol's length: 178 mm. Pistol's height: 120 mm. Pistol's width 32 mm. Barrel length: 113 mm.
Three safety devices: Magazine safety, safety catch and grip safety.

The Belgian Arms Factory manufactured this pistol for purely military use. The ring on the butt proves this.

One has to have had this brute in ones hand to fully realize its size. I have had just the model used in Paris at my disposal and done my experiments with it. I came rapidly to the conclusion that for suicide, especially for shooting through the heart, this weapon is the most inappropriate one can think of. It is too unwieldy; the barrel is too long. But above all the grip safety is difficult to operate as the pulling of the trigger and the disengaging of this safety device must be done simultaneously; otherwise the firing pin will not be released. Would anyone with a knowledge of firearms—as Ivar Kreuger had—buy such a weapon for a planned suicide?

My experiments with the FN-Browning, model 10/22 (see photograph) showed that a whole row of volonteers, who were otherwise conversant with firearms, could not shoot with the pistol. Not before they had become familiar with the special design of the grip safety could they handle the pistol, but none of them succeeded the first time in firing at their own hearts, with their left hands twisted round. The grip safety hinders the firing of the bullet when one shoots with a bent left hand; as in shooting towards ones own heart (see photograph).

I therefore consider it impossible for Ivar Kreuger, lying on his bed, to have shot himself through the heart with such a military weapon with his left hand. Based on my investigation of the facts and my experiments, I do not believe it was a case of suicide. And any criminologist in possession of experience and criminological compentence would not, at Ivar Kreugers death bed, have come to the conclusion that it was a case of suicide; but of murder".

Signed
Heinz Westphal
Kriminalhauptmeister

—

The report continues and criticizes the lack of professional investigation in Paris. It observes that the Frensch doctor can not see and/or follow the bullets penetration into the body. An additional observation made, is that Ivar Kreuger dressed fully before the shot was made. According to experience, most people undress to a certain extent if they are aiming a shot towards the body. However, most males chose to aim the gun at the head and only a very limited number aim at their heart.

The rule today seems to be that a criminologist, who from the beginning makes up his mind that the case is one of a suicide, without having checked all the facts, is acting irresponsibly.

Furthermore the report points out that those weapons found in the hands of a dead body are as a rule put there by a third pary. Therefore, a police investigator who finds a dead person with a gun or a knife in its hand has to act with extreme care as he no doubt will have to count with the possibility of a murder.

—

The following pictures speak for themselves. As you can see the tests do not tally with the description of the case that has been given by the authorities and been sent out all over the world by Kreuger's opponents. The pictures of the bullet wounds also speak for themselves. For me it is impossible to understand how anybody can say that they can not see the entrance and/or the bullets way into the body. But that might have been a part of the fake and the main reason why the autopsy was inhibited.

The type of pistol that was used in Paris.
Observe the grip safety.

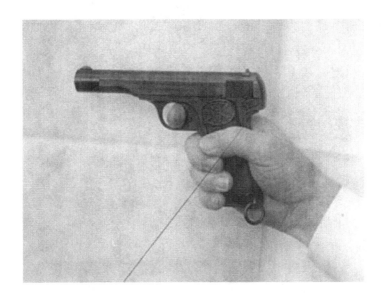

In this position the gun can not be fired.
The grip safety prevents it.

The gun must be held like this—in a firm grip
in order to be fired.

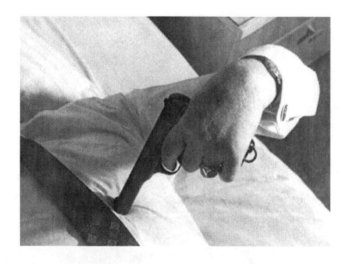

A shot towards the heart requires an unnatural angle of the hand.

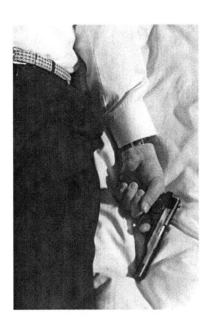 

It is possible to place a gun in a dead man's hand. The "grip" will be a very loose one as all muscles will be relaxed after the death. There are no informattion available about the exact position of Kreuger's hand when he was found. The pictures show the two alternatives. It is quite possible that Kreuger's stiff "triggerfinger" could have given the grip a cramped look.

If a gun is placed in a dead man's hand only a slight touch of the hand or arm will result in that the grip loosens and the gun slips out of the hand and will end up next to it.

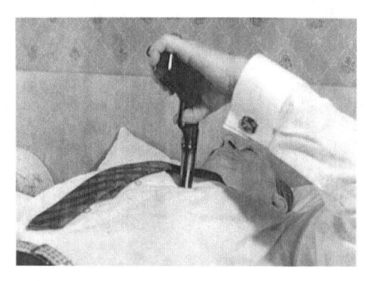

It is possible to use the thumb as "trigger finger" but it is difficult to get the necessary firm grip that is required. In the Krueger case you have to consider that he was fully dressed and that his normal "trigger finger" was stiff. The important question, however, is: What happens to the gun—where does it go?

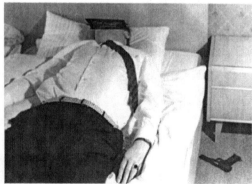

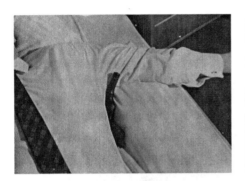

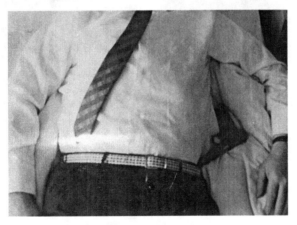

Observe that in none of the tests the gun has ended up as the police discribed the situation when **Ivar Kreuger** was found.

The Gunshot Wound

What does a gunshot wound look like? The Frensch doctor could not—according to his own report—see or follow the bullets entrance into the body.

In order to be able to show the reader what it looks like when a bullet of the caliber 9 mm (or close to it) hits a body, I needed help. A good friend of mine, Professor R. Swanson arranged access to pictures from an American expert on gunshot wounds, Dr. Vincent Di Maios, the author of GUNSHOT WOUNDS—Practical Aspects of Firearms, Ballistics and Forensic Techniques.

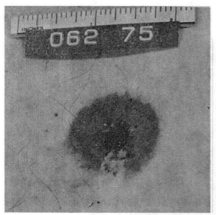 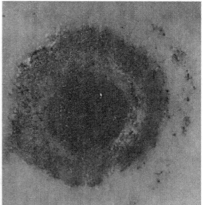

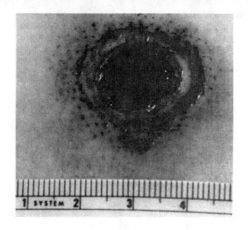

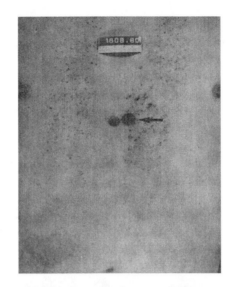

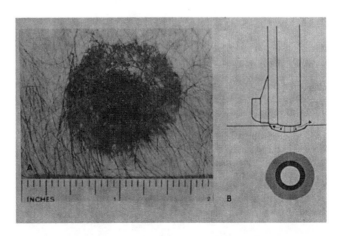

133

There is a considerable amount of information that a skilful investigator can get from studying a gunshot wound. If Kreuger had been shot there had to be an entrance hole and as the shot was fired at close range the hole should be possible to recognize—shouldn't it? Or was there no bullet hole but some other form of damage—as Dr. Lindquist thought—and was that the reason why an immediate autopsy was suggested? And in turn was this the reason why an autopsy in Paris as well as in Stockholm had to be avoided at any price?

If we number the pictures 1-6, the pictures 1, 2 and 4 shows the entrance whole from a 9 mm bullet from close range (contact shot). Picture nr 5 shows an entrance hole in the back from a smijacketed bullet. Picture nr 3 is of special interest as it shows how sootparticles have penetrated a shirt and are deposited on the body with the exception of the area that was covered with 4 layers of cloth i.e. the area in which the buttons are. No such observation was made in the Kreuger case. A considerable amount of soot should have been shown on the under-vest.

New Evidence

Interesting things that happened during the immediate period, prior and after the death of Ivar Kreuger.

My research in the Kreuger case is, as I have mentioned earlier, based on correspondence, telegrams and other documents that can be found in various archives.

I had for a long time tried to find out if there were telegrams filed from 1932 and if so if they were available for research. In the police archives there are telegrams but they are all copies and not originals. Therefore, I considered it to be an important step forward when I was informed via DSM (The Swedish Market) that there was an archive in Uppsala, which had a number of files under the name "The Kreuger Telegrams". Material, which as far as I knew, had not been studied before by other researchers on the subject. But apparently you can not be happy all the time. Many of the telegrams were in the form of "radio waves". A friend informed me that these waves were based on the Morse code and that the printing was called "Undulate printing". This of course made the telegrams very difficult to work with. First I had to learn the Morse code, which was not impossible but required quite some time. But that was not enough. The text in the telegrams was very often in the form of a cipher, grouped in five letters alternatively five figures. One of the difficulties in decoding—if you are not used to it—is to find where to grouping begins and with which letter or figure. Date, time, series number, number of the station etc. belongs to the telegram itself and differs not very much from the text. Another difficulty is that you more or less have to get to know the telegraph operator and his way of transmitting and the way it is received. The reason for this is that an A could possibly be E; U: W or T and a C could possibly be R; K; D or TR etc. As a group consist of five letters or figures there are as you can see quite a number of possible combinations. This in turn makes the decoding extremely time consuming. The picture below gives you an idea of what I was up against.

The last but not the least important thing is that you know which code or cipher you are working with. You do not feel much cleverer when you after some time of "translation" end up with "NATOV TJUJU". But almost every code has a codebook that works the same way as a dictionary. If you get the correct combination of the five letters and know which code it is (there are quite a number) then you can look it up and you will find that NATOV means "Sell at best" and TJUJY means $50.000:-.

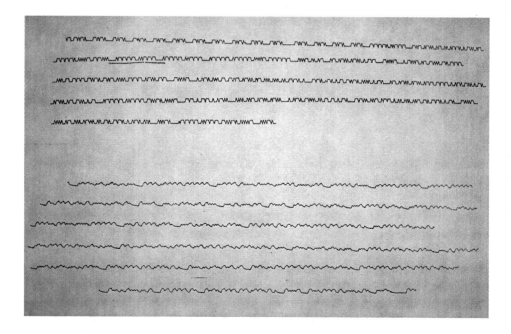

The upper part of the cable has been sent by a machine and the lower part by an operator by hand.

I am now going to present some of the telegrams that I consider to be of interest and at the same time tell what they prove. But before doing so, I have to introduce the reader to a couple of companies and in some cases also to their board members and some of their known and possible contacts.

Bank director Carl Frisk founded a company with the name of Société Financiére Suisse & Scandinave AB, in 1921*. For some reason it was going to be known as "Berth" which also became its cable address. The Board consisted of Carl Frisk, assistant secretary Fredrik von Dardel and H. Ashton.

We know the following about bank director Carl Frisk.

He was born November 20th 1865 and died of Cardiosclerosis on July 26th 1944 at an age of 78. He had an education in law and also in the mercantile subjects and did some practical work in Paris as well as London. In Sweden he worked with the following banks: Stockholms Intecknings Garanti AB; Stockholms Enskilda Bank and Stockholms Handelsbank (later Svenska Handelsbanken). He quit his work with Handelsbanken the same year that he founded his new company which had established agents in Geneva and Amsterdam already from the beginning. The intention was to market Swedish securities on the Swiss and Deutch markets. The company expanded quickly to Germany, England and the US. In 1931 the company had the following cable addresses registered: Berth; Berthenz; Byze; Dardel; Highberth and Hirts. In 1932 only Berth remained.

Carl Frisk was also dealing in real estate, art, jewellery and had an agent in Paris named Thor Carlander (TC).

- In the beginning of 1922 Marcus Wallenberg noted with satisfaction that Carl Frisk, director in Handelsbanken, had been pushed aside and was replaced by Mauritz Philipsson. In a letter to his youngest son dated February 1st 1922 MW writes that Frisk had had to withdraw as "he had always been telling lies like a raven" and that he had advanced "through ambition and hard work but failed on account of unreliability and vanity".

About Fredrik von Dardel we know:

He was born August 28th 1885. Studied law. He had several important positions in the Board of the Government Penal Institute; in the National Board of Health and the Karolinska Hospital. After 1932 he also got high positions in the Jubilee Funds of King Oscar II and King Gustav V. He was married to Maria Sophia Wising in her second marriage. It could be said that Dardel became indirectly related to the Wallenbergs through marriage. Dardel does not seem to have been very active in the company. However, he probably filled an important part through his contacts with Wallenberg. He might also have been one of the persons that visited Governor Nils Edén in connection with the inhibition of the autopsy of Ivar Kreuger. Dardel, however, comes into the picture once more.

On March 30th 1934 Fredrik von Dardel most probably wrote a very remarkable letter, addressed to a person in Oslo, Norway. Unfortunately the name of the addressee has been removed. The letter reads:

"With reference to our telephone conversation I herewith, on behalf of bank director Wallenberg, want to inform that Broblewsky now has returned to his legal domicile. No trouble can occur as B. himself no longer is here and investigations with K. have ended"

If Fredrik von Dardel really wrote this letter—it is his signature—then we can make some interesting observations.

Through the letter we get a more direct link between "Berth" and the Wallenbergs in a very delicate question. Dardel's positions could also have made it possible for him to save Erik Sjöström (Managing Director of K&T) from the police interrogation and instead to be heard and directed by Hugo Stenbeck (This part is dealt with on pages 292/293 in my first book).

There is not much to be said about the third person on the Board, H. Ashton. He seems to have been the one who handled the daily work in the company.

Carl Frisks connections with Josef Sachs.

Karl L Lundberg was the owner of the largest department store in Stockholm in the beginning of 1900. Lundbergs daughter was married to Carl Frisk. Sachs owned a somewhat smaller department store under the name Leja. Josef Sachs wife and Lundbergs daughter were childhood friends. The two families, Sachs and Frisk became close friends. Josef Sachs asked Frisk to investigate if Mr. Lundberg could be interested in a merger between their two stores in order to create an even larger department store.

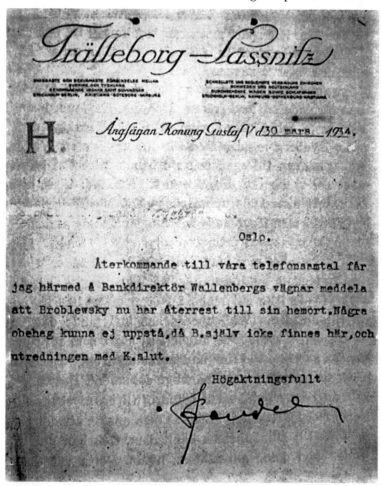

Fredrik von Dardels letter March 30th 1934.

The merger resulted in NK (Nordiska Kompaniet). At the preliminary Board Meeting, that was held on January 14th 1902 the following persons were present: Karl L Lundberg; Josef Sachs; Abr. Nachmanson; Arthur Thiel, Carl Frisk and Walter Philipson. The share capital was set to 2,700.000 Crowns.

The 29th of September 1924, Société Finansiére pour Valeures Scandinave en Suisse, was founded and got the working name SUSCA. The share capital was paid in by Erik Sjöström (K&T). One Mr. Dardel in Geneva ran the company. Possibly, he was a relative of Fredrik von Dardel. Carl Frisk was also on the Board of this company. You will find the company listed in the bankruptcy documents in the estate of Kreuger & Toll.

There are no direct connections between Carl Frisk and Ivar Kreuger during the last years. However, during the developing period of Kreuger & Toll they probably had a lot to do with each other in connection with mortgages and other financing for building and contracting projects. Through notes from the police archive you can see that Kreuger and Frisk had lunch together at an average of once a year.

Cables, extracts from letters, police investigations and incidents most of them not previously published

Extract from a letter December 10th 1931 from Frisk to Dardel, Geneve.

"Regarding Kreuger's visit to Bern and what might have been the reason for this visit I called and asked Sjostrom. Sjostrom had no knowledge what so ever of Kreuger having been to Bern and did not know of any reason why he should have gone there".

This letter shows that everyone kept an eye on Kreuger's doings. The contacts between Frisk and Sjostrom seemed to be rather good. Possibly Kreuger had suspected this and did not inform Sjostrom of more sensitive negotiations.

Cable 01.27.1932 15.09
SWK 401 New York 12 W
LCO=Gronberg telegrambolaget STKM. When can I get figures for LM Ericsson. Kreugivar

Kreugivar was Kreugers cable address. It is interesting to find that Kreuger asks for the yearly figures for LM Ericsson as it shows that he was not responsible for those or the book keeping as such.

01.27.1932 extract from notes for the police archive.

"On an oral order from Sjostrom 01.27.1932 100.000 and then 3.2.1932 an additional 150.000 debentures were turned over to "Berth". All blocks noted below have been sold and Kreugers account credited:

02.12.1932	38.656:02	Nom. Kr 20.000
02.17. 1932	108.946:06	Nom. Kr 50.000
02.18. 1932	42.535:85	Nom. Kr 20.000
03.10. 1932	26.992:-	Nom. Kr 14.000
03.10. 1932	17.256:75	Nom. Kr 9.000
03.12. 1932	32.977:33	Nom. Kr 20.000

The remaining Nom 17.000 participating debentures remained in depot with Berth"

Now, the last sentence of the above statement is not quite true. On 12.3.1932 at 12.28 Berth received the following cable:

"Urgent hirts shlm Sold 17800 5, 6700 51/8 closed nazne balance follows" ("nazne" means here speculation).

A little later the same day Berth gets another cable:
"sold 5500 5, completes turnover 165400"

This indicates very good contacts between Sjostrom and Frisk when such large amounts of debentures are turned over based on "oral orders".

03.14. 1932
To Schéle Matches Stkm
"Have exact information regarding French newspaper campaign against the company call Grand Hotel—Ostelius"

The cable was sent from Paris. This is an interesting proof for the campaigns directed at the Kreuger Group. It is also of interest that it is addressed to Schéle as legal procedures had already begun in Paris.

02.14. 1932
Extract from a letter from TC (Paris) to Frisk
"The attacks against Kreuger Group are from financial papers belonging to the "Chantage class" such as for example Mme Hanans "Force".

It was interesting to find that above cable to Schéle also was found in the archive of Carl Frisk. Apparently Schéle had told some contacts that he also could be reached through Frisk.

02.16. 1932
Hogmanus STKM
2,335.000 kronor nominna K&T obligations laying in depot for your account.
Bourphal

The cable is sent to the banker A V Hogman confirming the amount of bonds that have been placed in his account. Mr Hogman never accounted for this amount neither for any other. Neither the investigators nor the administrators did go after Hogman in order to retrieve any of the funds.

Jonas Angstrom

Cable from Berth 4 to Susca Geneve = Pay Thursday bankverein for account nineteen sthlm hundred thousand.

"Nineteen Sthlm" is the cable address of Stockholms Enskilda Bank. Berth just requests Susca to pay 100.000 to the Swiss bank "Bankverein" for the account of Stockholms Enskilda Bank.

Extract from a letter dated March 1st 1932 from T.C. (Paris) to Frisk:
  "Otherwise I have nothing of interest to report except that I heard yesterday from Cederschöld that certain baisse-parties once more have begun to operate against the securities of the Kreuger Group. I assume that it is the same consortium that works along the same lines from Switzerland.

The real interest of this letter is to show how people close to Kreuger "spill" information and how there was a constant "fishing" for news with regard to Kreuger and the Kreuger Group.

Extract from a letter dated March 4th 1932 from Dardel to Frisk
  "The turnover in Paris continues to be enormous. The Stock Exchange is completely disorganized and many securities are not quoted while it is open. The brokers are 4 to 6 days behind with their service. Today there was a large profit taking without lower rates. I believe that the international professionals that now take their profits in Paris will transfer their hausse operations to New York and later on to the smaller European exchanges such as Amsterdam and Stockholm. But I believe that the tendency has turned.

This supports what has been said earlier. Tremendous amounts of Kreuger securities were being sold and those who were speculating against him were getting into an increasingly difficult situation. If the tendency had turned, and optimism were to return to the International Markets, there would be trouble. How to get out of that became a bigger and bigger problem.

Cable. 3.5.32 (*March 5, 1932*)
Kibeak pour Hoffman Istanbul
IK sailed yesterday from New York arriving Paris 10th
Bergman
  Hoffman was responsible for the Turkish monopol and was also an important link to Italy. As far as I have been able to find out Hoffman had no appointments with Kreuger. Neither was he in Paris March 11th or 12th, at least not officially. The cable is giving the wrong date of arrival.

3.5.32
To Berth from Amsterdam 17.15
CXEGI XRAEM UHGRY PKCIO—WERTMA
Confirm New York City sold 500 shares 7

142

3.5.32
To JAPO (Jacobson & Ponsbach) Stkm
Ausliefert Berth mark 50.000 sechsenihalber Bayerische Vereinsbank mark 50.000
Bayeriche Hypoteken gegen zahlung von kronen 100.000—Trahanba

The above two cables show that Berth is in business contact with those companies that Littorin mentions in his cable of 29.4.31 as baisse speculators.

3.8.32 Berth 69 16.50
Hirts New York
SELEA CHTHO PEPHZ SHORT
(16.050 bonds (?) short)

3.8.32 from Ö-m 8308
=D=Hirts New York
7 sell twothousand kreuger short

The number given above is a telephone number registered in the name of the private banker Alfred Berg.

3.9.32
Berth 78 17.05
    Enesto New York = vorschlagen vorgebet bis 3000 kreuger falls effekten und deviesen nicht stark verändert—Berth

Berth also works with short selling for its German customers.

3.9.32 15.10
BACOCHASE New York
RLUIF URMTI XVEGO URMTI LOEBCARL ODVYE UJYIK TJUET TIWCI XUBSE.
    Pay to Wertheim & Co for our account to carl loeb 1500 stop receive for our account $47.775 from Hirch Lilienthal & Co

Wertheim & Co was a company in New York that according to Littorin was a member of the international chain that was operating against the Kreuger Group.

3.9.32
New York 22.51
NLT Hirts Sthlm
    Vorgaben ingesamt funfzehnhundert 6 7/8 funfzehnhundert 6 3/4 Clardodge Hents hirlico grossere abgeber GLABE KRT. Keine grosse baisseposition—Ernesto

Short selling confirmed.

3.9.32 from Norr 7959 10.20
Byard Bourse for Ferriere Paris
    Please pay Mr Tage Lundberg Grand Hotel at visite Friday twelve at half past ten oclock and you will receive 3000 for hundred 5500 for fourty and 10000 for twenty. Egnal

I have so far not been able to make very much out of this cable. The telephone number of the sender is registered on wholesaler H P Greiszen. It is signed Egnal which is the cable address of the private banker Mr. Lange. Friday was not the 12ᵗʰ but the 11ᵗʰ.

3.10.32 13.15 Berth 84
BACOCHASE New York
RIBSU JAUIX FIECT TJYAG XTYYO YEKNY
    380 pay on Friday to Guarantee Trust Co of New York for account Sodermanlands Enskilda Bank 560.000

Check cable dated 3.12.32.

3.10.32
Paris 21/20 w 18.30
Egnal Sthlm
    Sending you today cheque 1,500,000 stop have remitted Schéle on his request 10,000 pounds from your account.—Bayard

This cable has a certain interest as it shows that Schéle received £ 10, 000 from the account of the private banker Karl Lange just upon his own request. I have not been able to find that Schéle accounted for this money. £10,000 was quite a bit of money in those days.

We are now getting close to the crucial time. The flood of cables does increase quite a bit and I have not by far been able to decode all of them. My intention has only been to show that a lot of short selling existed; that the short selling increased the 11ᵗʰ and 12ᵗʰ of March; and that there was an increase in sales about and just after the time when Kreuger was shot. I wanted to show who was behind the large transactions in Stockholm and New York that nobody has been able to disclose, as nobody took the time to locate and decipher the telegrams.

Extract from a letter dated 11ᵗʰ March 1932 from Dardel to Frisk Regarding the annual reports for Susca and Berth.
    "It would be nice if they could be finished as soon as possible with all these crazy rumors around Kreuger. "He should have shot himself after that he had taken 10

million from the cashier. Wallenberg had forced him to resign. He would never return to Sweden but stay in America and so on." It would be good to be able to show that Susca's and Berth's accounts are in order and unchallengeable."

There were fantastic rumors that were spread all over. Interestingly enough the persons spreading them have chosen the information that Kreuger shot himself. There are other ways that you can take your life. The link to Wallenberg also has its interest.

3.11.32 from London
    Berthswiss Sthm = Bitte sendet alle meta match hieher report unmöglich.

Again a somewhat cryptic cable which could be interpreted so that the sender want all match securities that had been transacted for their joint account. However, it is not possible to report. Why?

3.11.32
From Berth 95 (previously published in DSM)
    =Credionnais Paris = 1450 avisez et payez Leon Birthschansky 281 Rue Saint Honore compte Carl Frisk seizemille 16,000 francs= Berth

Carl Frisk was not only working on the Stock Market but bought and sold real estate, art and jewelry and other valuables. Leon Birthschansky was an art dealer in Paris. The payment of 16,000 francs could very well be for a picture or two but could also be the payment for some other kind of service.

What happened on March 11th 1932?

Ivar Kreuger arrived in Paris

Ivar Kreuger informed his brother Torsten Kreuger over the phone that he had full evidence against those who had been working against him.

Schéle was the only outsider that overheard Kreuger's telephone conversation. (If we exclude the possibility that someone is listening on the line).

Sune Schéle's relatives begin to sell debentures.

Uppland's Enskilda Bank registers that they are doing business with debentures—with Ivar Kreuger.

Wermlandsbanken registers that they are doing business with debentures—with Ivar Kreuger.

Director E. Sjostrom sells a large block of STAB to Wermlandsbanken.

Sune Schéle's transactions are marked with "strictly confidential" in red in the police archive.

(The above information has been obtained from the police archives)

A gun is bought under mysterious circumstances. (see page 58)

3.12.1932

Ivar Kreuger dies some time between 11.30-12.10

The relatives of Sune Schéle continue to sell debentures.

Wermlandsbanken is making large transactions in debentures—with Ivar Kreuger.

Upplandsbanken is also making large transactions in debentures—with Ivar Kreuger.

E Sjostrom sells another large block of STAB to Wermlandsbanken.

Ivar Kreuger possibly writes a letter to Littorin in order to explain certain information given to Donald Durant of Lee Higginson, onboard the ship from New York.

Josef Sachs is interviewed by the two principal Swedish newspapers and gives them false information.

(Information about the transactions in securities comes from the police archives)

We know that Ivar Kreuger definitely did not sell any debentures to the two banks, neither on Friday nor on Saturday. The transactions might have been done in connection with collateral (with or without the right to do so), or in order to cover short transactions. The interesting thing is that these transactions are made the same day that Kreuger dies.

3.12.32 fr New York NLT

Hirts Sthm = final report sold altogether vostro 3000 5 1/4 7900 5 1/8 2600 5 sold jointly 1000 5 1/4 market generally dull Kreuger news not known during market here. Hentz also heavy seller wire Monday earliest.

This cable is of great interest as it shows that Berth and Hentz sold in New York before the American markets were informed about the death of Ivar Kreuger. Even with consideration taken to the time difference the order must have been placed rather early Saturday the 12th.

3.12.32 Fr Berlin

Berthenz Stockholm = sold fourthousandfivehundred debentures 525 fourthousandfourhundred 5125 seventhousandonehundred 5255

3.12.32 Berthswiss London 13.30

Verkauften 40.000 debentures 128.60 jetzt unser konkurrenz Hägglöf verkaufer zu 128 (Another cable at 14.20)

Verkauften 30.000 debentures 127.60 ingesamt 70.000

3.12.32

New York 12.28 (stamped 1932 March 12th pm 6.30)

Urgent Hirts Sthlm (Berth)

Sold 17899 5 6700 5 1/8 closed NAZNE balance follows.

(Another cable at 12.56)

Sold 5500 5 completes turnover 165 400

Above mentioned cables are only extracts out of a large number of cables from Berths activity during March 12th 1932. I hope that I will be able to decode the remaining cables but these are enough to prove an unusually high turnover and activity just before the death of Ivar Kreuger is announced officially. It is also of interest to observe that Hägglöf, who was close to Stockholms Enskilda Bank more or less, dumps debentures. The cable sent from London corresponds quite well with the time when Kreuger was found dead.

3.12.32 from New York (probably sent March 11 as night letter)

Bertloeb Sthm = spreading confidence reflected in strength domestic foreign bonds and success new government and utility financing stop expect narrow fluctuations stock market pending advent improved business stop would purchase on weakness.

Cable shows a calm market in America.

3.12.32 Berth 127 15.20

D=Hirts New York=Sehr nervous NZNHZ vorschlagen nichts machen abwarten Hindenburg.

Someone got nervous about their short selling.

3.12.32 Berth 122 13.55

BACOCHASE New York

RAYFV UJYIK TJIEP TIVIR XUBSE ODVYVE UJYIK ABFJU TJASU LOEBCARL LAOKD ODVYV UJYIK TJJOY XUBER ODVYV JAUIX IETWX TJZEI XTYYO YEKNY

261 received for our account $22,550 from Hirch, Lilienthal & Co stop received for our account about $5000 from loebcarl acknowledge receipt of cable stop received for our account $30,000 from H. Hentz & Co stop pay to Guarantee Trust of New York $70,000 for account of Södermanlands Enskilda Bank on Monday.

Paying off loans? Possibly accounting for short sales. Note that the time the cable was sent is very shortly after Kreuger was found dead. This information was not yet official.

3.12.32 Fr nitton 536 18.05

=D= Wallenberg Grandhotel Cannes = Ivar hastigt avlidit Paris stop junior hemkommer morgon bittida underrätta om Eder närvaro anses erforderlig— Calissendorf.

Ivar suddenly died in Paris stop junior returning early tomorrow inform if your presence considered necessary—Calissendorf

Junior in this case means Jacob Wallenberg who was in London. It is interesting to note the time. Kreuger's death was officially announced earlier and you would have expected an immediate reaction from Stockholms Enskilda Bank.

3.13.32 Fr Storlien 15.20

Sune Schele bristonore Paris 109

Telegrafera fristedt att ovillkorligen lösa lånen i skaraborgsbanken med försålda debentures.

Ragnar

Cable Fristedt (a broker) to unconditionally pay the loans in Skaraborgsbanken with revenues from sold debentures.

3.13.32 20.35

Paris Fr 33 38 W

Schéle, Storlien Suede

You have sold in your name and Fristedt have no right whatsoever to refuse follow you instructions have told them so over the telephone and advise you insist on you rights legally if necessary.

Sune

There seems to be unrest on the market and some brokers either refused to deal with debentures or withheld the proceeds.

Extract from the press.
DN (Dagens Nyheter) 3.12.32 (written about the conditions March 11)
Apart from the worries about the result of the German election, it was the pessimistic rumors about the Kreuger Group/s possibility to pay dividends and the weak quotes in New York that brought about large sales from a lot of various sources. The market got weaker and was followed by sales from abroad. Kreuger debentures were paid 153-149 and finished 151-141.

Sunday March 13th 1932
The following was reported from leading American stockbrokers in Paris with regard to Ivar Kreuger's suicide.
"The death of Ivar Kreuger has been kept a secret until after the close of the New York Stock Exchange, 5 o'clock Paris time and 6 o'clock middle European time. This was also made easy as the Exchange in Paris was closed today on account of the burial ceremony of Briand."

3.13.32 (written about the conditions 3.12)
Kreuger panic on the Stock Exchange
More than 15,000 debentures were thrown into the market yesterday. 10,000 during trading hours but 15,600 for the whole day. Forced sales. There were especially sales from two sources—a broker and a bank—that pressed the quotes to a new low for the year. There was also a large turnover in STAB. The after market carried great nervousness and excitement. B-debentures were in parity with the New York rates that were 134, but after increased selling the quotes fell to 130. A great part of the large quantities of debentures were probably sold at this rate. After business hours the rates continued to fall to a low of 125.

Kreuger sale in New York
Debentures $5. The Stock Exchange stable. The exception was Kreuger & Toll with a large turnover at a somewhat lower rate. This was partly caused by the fact that ITT was not going to pay any dividend and the weak markets, where this company was working.

3.13.32
From Berth 137
=Credionnais Paris= 1441 notre letter 12 bonifiez 200000 franc handelsbank valeur 14/3 aulieu 15/3 priere avisez handelsbank telegraphiquement demain matain=Berth

3.13.32
Fr Berth 138
SUSCA fuer Dardel Geneve

Betala samtliga francbelopp för försålda Kreuger till Credionnais i stället för Birka

Pay all franc amounts for sold Kreuger to Credit Lyonnais instead of Birka.

The 13th of March 1932 was a Sunday but Berth seems to have been in a great hurry to take certain actions such as moving assets to a completely free standing foreign bank.

March 13th—less than 24 hours after Kreuger death things begin to happen also in Stockholm. The lawyer Hugo Stenbeck gets in touch with the director of Kreuger & Toll, Erik Sjostrom and makes it clear to him that the position of the Board was such that they were in need of immediate legal assistance and help which he was willing to supply. The acting of Hugo Stenbeck—now and later—is rather confusing. Who asked him for advice? Personally I do not think it is wrong to see a link between him and the other interests that wanted to remove Ivar Kreuger. And there is no question that Stenbeck belonged to the Group that gained the most on Kreuger's death.

Monday 14th March 1932 (Dagens Nyheter, page 4)
   "In his talks with his American friends in the banking business as well as during his visit to the White House Kreuger had been very optimistic about his European and American companies. He did not, which was underlined in a communiqué from the bankers Lee Higginson, look for any loans in America. American people of finance, in general, also confirmed this. Kreuger knew very well that the times for loans were very difficult and only could be arranged at costs and conditions that would be to a great disadvantage."

———

"It has not been possible to disclose if sales orders came from sources that in advance knew about the death"

(Someone at least thought about the possibility)

———

"Also according to the quotes at the end of the trading, certificates were 1/4 dollar above the low from January 5th".

———

"Wall Street considered the Kreuger Group's situation neither better nor worse than the one of ITT or Foreign Power Co and was expecting suspended dividends."

3.14.32 Paris

Lauritzen Karlavägen 1 Sthm

Referring request obtain cooperation New York London Paris Amsterdam and Swiss exchanges to suspend all dealings in our securities for two days our friends endeavoring bring this about but all of them sir Guy Granet Hallowell and Durant feel sure by far the best way is to have Stockholm exchange officials telegraph their request direct to various exchange presidents stop you will realize that such request from private parties and particularly from parties who might be considered interested may not prove effective. Littorin

3.14.32

Hugo Stenbeck is not resting. On Monday the 14th he divides—at his own home— the assignments to all the lawyers in Stockholm to represent members of the Kreuger Group. Also people that had been close to the Group were to be represented. The lawyers in question were of course those that were expected to follow the lines of Stenbeck and his principals.

3.15.32

Hugo Stenbeck and his partner Olle Ohlsén summons a meeting in Ivar Kreuger's private office in the Swedish Match Company at 07.00 a.m. The notice is not signed.

Question: By what right? On who's order or wish?

At the meeting the two lawyers took possession of Ivar Kreuger's private safe where, among other things, the documents regarding the Italian monopoly were kept. Of course they did not make a list over the contents of the safe. According to a police record from March 1933 bank director Oscar Rydbeck had sent a cable from the train from Paris and demanded that all Kreuger's offices as well as his private apartment should be sealed. Only authorized persons in the company of witnesses should be allowed to enter. The police record states that all documents that had been brought out had been duly and orderly registered. Police activity was questionable and depended on who's orders they were working at the time.

Wednesday March 16th (Dagens Nyheter, page 12)

New York

The Kreuger Group had only a smaller commercial loan, divided over several banks and well covered. It is maintained that the credit is only for $9 million dollars. The bankers Lee Higginson, who always have been identified with Kreuger & Toll, had only a small engagement as the bank has cut its interest in the Kreuger Group during the last year. Those who were initiated have known the financial structure of the Swedish Group for months wherefore the suicide will not change the opinion.

151

3.15.32
Berth 166 17.15 Swissbourse Geneva
Bestätigen kauften 7000 debentures 57 glattstelten valuta 98

3.15.32 16.30
Schweizesbank Zurich
Bestätigen kauften 40.000 debentures 54 175 Kreugerb. 4350 185 Match A 54 verkauften
40.000 francs 98 Berth

3.15.32
Suissbourse Geneva
Bestätigen kauften 23000 debentures 54 glattställten valuta 98—Berth 3.15.32 to Berth
15.24 from Amsterdam
343 hersendet ex depot kronen zehnthousand debentures Kreutolls—Trahanba

3.15.32to Berth 19.00 from Amsterdam
427 hersendet ex depot hundert match B—Trahanba

Berth is buying large quantities of Kreuger securities. Is this In order to cover short sales or replace collateral?

3.16.32
DDD Paris 06 19/18 w 12.34
Urgent Egnal Sthlm = Schéle ask us to remit him 400,000 kronor debentures stop can
we do it?—Bayard

Egnal cable address for Karl H Lange. Schéle asks for a large block of debentures. For what purpose? Is this to cover short sales or replace collateral? This time Mr. Lange is asked if the transaction could be carried out. Previously Schéle took out £10, 000 upon his own request.

3.16.32 SIGAB (Stockholm Intecknings Garantiaktiebolag) sends the following cable
to Lee Higginson in Boston.

NASLUPOMEY TKFOIUYMZB NASLUPOKYW TKIBOTJRUO UYMXZNASLU
POKKITJIXI VBADINASLU PIAVBTJOUT VEOVDNASLU PKKEUTKAKO
VEOYGNASLU PIAPWTKIBO VEOXFIWERC SIGAB

This is an order to Lee Higginson to sell Belgian, Danish and German bonds for a total sum of nom. $480,000. The order is valid until executed. So far I have not been able to determine if the order concerns collateral or deposited securities. Probably it was not *quite legal as K&T had received moratorium March 14th and was under the control of the Government.*

3.16.32 11.05 Berth 175

Stornierbar kauften 30.000 debentures 5050

-46 vornahmen 50.000 debentures 29 vornahmen 200 Kreugerb.

13.00	nahmen weiter hundertausen debentures 45.58
13.35	stornieren 150.000 debentures
45.45	Kauften 20.000 debentures 43.50
14.00	Bestätigen nahmen 60.000 debentures 43.50
25.25	Bestätigen kauften 55.000 debentures 43 150 aktien 2650
20.20	Bestätigen kauften 82000 debentures 4225 150 kreuger b 2050
18.35	Bestätigen kauften 14000 debentures 38.25

3.16.32 Berth 208

17.15 Schweizerbank Zurich Kauften 100 kreugerb 2250—Berth

16.40 Bestätigen kauften 250 Match B

15.25 Bestätigen kauften 30.000 debentures 42.25

12.05 Bestätigen verkauften 70.000 debentures 46 stop Kauften 10.000 44.50 kauften 400 kreugerb 29

Berth

3.16.32 Berth 182

= Berthswiss London = nahmen weiter hundertthausand debentures 4550

On March 16th Berth continues to buy large quantities of Kreuger securities. We do not know yet if they were for the cover of short sales or for the replacement of sold collaterals.

3.16.32 Berth 190 14.30

Berthhenz New York

RAVAW UJYIK UWGYI VIOWM XVEGO UJYIK UWIJP UWICI UWFSE VIOWM XUIGE OJASC KBGEU EUYUW ODVYE URONZ TJOUT XTYYO

227 received for our account 1,000 shares K&T from Wertheim & Co received for our account 50,400 shares from Lee Higg. Short position even or there about stop pay for our account $140,000 to Guarantee Trust Co of NY

Berth is closing a short position.

3.16.32 Berth 206 17.05

BACOCHASE New York

RKIUL DUCAY OUHMB YEKOZ TJOUT BSIAL YEKOZ
408 credit value to day Stockholms Enskilda Bank $40,000 please cable SEB.

3.16.32 17.10
GUARASUDIS New York
(Same text as per above, signed Berth 206)

Berth is transferring a total amount of 2 x $40,000 = $80,000 to Stockholms Enskilda Bank. The transfer could be a payment for sold collateral, payment for the financing of a short sale, or payment for a short sale for the banks own account or for the account of one of their clients. The sum of $80,000 was quite a bit of money in 1932. Whatever the exact meaning of the cable it gives us another link between Berth and Stockholms Enskilda Bank (SEB).

3.16.32 14.30
GUARASUDIS New York
UJYIK TKIBO TJOUT XUBER JYXEG LAOKD
Received for our account $140,000 from H Henz & Co please acknowledge receipt of cable

3.16.32 15.35
BACO CHASE New York
UJYIK TJOFE XVEGO JYXEG LAOKD
    Received for our account from Wertheim & co $35,000 please acknowledge receipt of cable.

Berth is closing some quite considerable deals in New York.

3.16.32
March 16th Hugo Stenbeck gets in touch with the Minister of Finance, Felix Hamrin, with the information that the board of director of Kreuger & Toll has elected an investigators' committee consisting of Jacob Wallenberg, Ernfrid Browaldh, Martin Fehr, Torsten Nothin and Bjorn Prytz. After this meeting Hugo Stenbeck went to the board of directors of K&T and told them that the Government had nominated a commission consisting of the above mentioned persons with the purpose of assisting in the investigating of Kreuger & Tolls financial position. When this daring move is made Stenbeck is very careful not to have his own name mentioned.

3.17.32 21.50 64 Sthlm 17902 9
Hotel Wessler Charlotenburg Berlin
Zimmer mit einem bett—Bergenstråhle

For some reason Bergenstråhle books a room with one bed in Berlin. Berlin was where some of Kreuger's opponents met on the way home from France. Berlin was also the place where it was

The Murder of Ivar Kreuger

thought that the train with Kreuger's coffin would pass. A last minute change sent that part of the train via Hamburg.

3.17.32 Berth 220 12.50
Schweizerbank Zurich
Bestätigen kauften 50.000 debentures 32.50 stop kauften 300 kreugerb 18—Berth

11.45
Bestätigen kauften 100 kreugerb 13—Berth
Kauften 35 Kreugerb 141 110 Match B 90.35—Berth

3.17.32 Berth 83
Berthswiss London
Kauften 100,000 debentures 3,50—Berth 221

17.3.32
Berthswiss London Berth 214
Transferieren heute 100,000 debentures—Berth

Berth continues to buy large quantities of Kreuger securities. Judging from the amounts there must have been large short transactions or deposited collateral that had to be restored.

3.17.32 Paris 16.35
Matchco pour Ekstroem Sthkm
    Alla papper och handlingar av vad slag vara må ävensom penningar och personliga nipper medfördes av Littorin stop i våningen finns endast kläder ett par möbler samt några bibelots av föga värde stop jag känner intet kassafack i hans namn stop skall fråga Schele.
Cederschiöld

All papers and documents of what ever kind there is, money and personal belongings were taken by Littorin stop in the apartment there are only suits some furniture and books of no value stop I know of no safe in his name stop will ask Schéle—Cederschiöld

Apparently things were utterly confused at the time. All documents were according to information sent with Miss Bokman. This is confirmed by police record and by a witness hearing in the Stockholm Lower Court as late as 1958. In no archives is it mentioned that Littorin had any documents with him when he returned. The information "no safe in his name" is of no interest. If Kreuger had had a safe or safe deposit box, it would either be a numbered account or in a close associate or relatives' name. In this connection it is worth noting that the pistol, which it is maintained that Kreuger had bought, was not sent to Sweden. No license was required in France

155

at that time and the gun was supposed to be Kreuger's. As we know Kreuger owned quite a number of handguns in Sweden and if a license or permit of any kind was required they were probably in order. The correct thing would have been to send the gun and ammunition to the Swedish police for the estate's account. It is however, quite possible that the French authorities accepted the fact that the gun was not bought by Ivar Kreuger.

3.17.1932
   Miss Bokman returns to Sweden with three suitcases, sealed by the Swedish Legation. They contained Ivar Kreuger's private documents, which he had brought back from New York. As you can see the information given by Cederschiöld (above) is not correct.

3.17.1932 Lee Higginson sends the following cable:
   The cable seems to have been sent to Stockholms Intecknings Garantiebolag, which handled financial matters with Lee Higginsson.

BURPO AOFTE OIWHY ANAZT DAIUS JRYGM DFYYZ ITTCE JOLYE MDAMO EAHXV OXIKD IDLAN ITOXH OLMEU PACOY ALIYT GVIDI KAEBR KLOGY OJBIR FEMGA JEWUM IPVGY OVUCU AJZRE LBCEY FIOGC FIIVD ODVYE KFYAO PASDN GIFYK IEKFX EZOWD NFUSI IPULF EBIKI OXLHU LVIOJ FIKOD EZUWT JAYGM IPDNO OXIKD IDLAN KLOGY DYXSI IGEIR ARMFI ESKON ALFYD JEWUM IPOGY BYBSE FVYGI AIZRE ARMYB FIVKU ODVYE CVORU HEIWU OHCUC ONHAE FIEEV NWUTO IDOFM IONWZ IXDAP FEUBG AGVKA KAEBR

Decoded:

Can we assume that we are to continue to pay coupon(s) on your 5% secured debentures which matured on 1st of March year 1932 and on interest date(s) please read the proceeding word in plural prior thereto for payment(s) of which we have already received funds (SF) from you stop presume you have in mind extreme seriousness of default(s) which would results from failure(s) to pay obligations which matured prior dates moratorium became effective and for payment of which cash has already been furnished stop please confirm not later than 8.30 a.m. our time Friday forenoon so that we may notify our foreign agent(s) please read preceding word in plural.

Higginson

There were rumors that told that Kreuger could not pay the interest coupon on the secured debentures. Those who maintained that did not bother to read this cable in clear text. Or possibly, they did not know how to. As far as I know the cable was not given any official announcement. Nor have I seen any information about how the money was handled?

3.18.32 Paris 17.20

Matchco Stockholm

Schéle cables from Hanover that the car with the remains of the boss during the night was disconnected and directed to Hamburg instead of Berlin stop the railway authorities here have assured the expected time of arrival in Stockholm will not be changed stop have informed Hallstrom stop advice to check with Trelleborg if the car passes Saturday 6.20 Drachenfels

In the book "Ivar Kreuger Murdered?" by Borje Heed and Sven Stolpe, they speculated that the coffin was removed from the church in which it was kept upon its arrival to Sweden. The church has made an investigation and arrived at the conclusion that it was impossible for the coffin to leave the crypt during the time in question. I have visited the church and found that even if the coffin had not left the church, it would have been possible to remove and return its contents without creating any commotion. This does not in any way mean that something like that happened. The above-mentioned cable however, shows that the coffin during the transportation to Sweden, during a certain period of time, went some other way than what had been planned from the beginning. It did not get to Berlin where Bergenstrahle went and anything could have happened during this transport. Just what, if anything, we will probably never know. The whole discussion emanates from the rumor that a secret autopsy might have been made.

3.18.32 Swissbourse Geneva

Bestätigen kauften Meta 40.000 debentures 38.25—Berth

3.18.32 15.25 Schwizerbank Zurich

Bestätigen kauften 50.000 debentures 38.25

3.18.32—Schweizerbank Zurich

Kauften 350 kreugerb 2325 350 2125 400 20,25 295 Match B 52.50

3.18.32 Berth 251

15.45 Berth Swiss London

Akzeptieren kauften 10.000 38.25

16.20 Accord kauften 20.000 debentures 38.25

Berth continuous to buy large block of Kreuger securities. Again, the question arises about the purpose?

3.18.32 from Riga 14.57

LCO = Pomatum New York

Bitte uberweiset drahtlich meinen gunsten dreitausendfymfhundert dollar Riga Internationalbank Riga Commerzbank undienlich.

Morkreuger

So far I have not been able to decode and trace either the sender or the addressee in New York. However, it is quite clear that somebody wants his monthly $3500 dollar.

3.18.32 Swiss bank Geneva

Please sell best possible without spoiling the market the securities for our loan eight hundred shares and six hundred debentures Kreutolls
AWEASA

The private banker A W Hogman is trying to sell some of the assets that were deposited with him.

3.18.32

The 18th of March 1932—one week after Kreuger's arrival to Paris from New York—turned out to be an eventful day. The lawyers Stenbeck and Ohlsén came to STAB's office in order to meet Miss Bokman. They introduced themselves as being members of the investigators' committee and broke the seals on all the suitcases that contained Ivar Kreuger's papers. Stenbeck took all the documents that he believed were of interest as well as all of Ivar Kreuger's note books. Stenbeck confessed to this theft in Court 1958 when the crime since long had been barred by the statute of limitation. Now, a very interesting thing happens. Miss Bokman, who is a witness to what the lawyers are doing, can not remember what happened to the suitcases when she had left them in STAB's office. Neither does she remember to whom she might have given them. She gave these statements in Court shortly after her return. Roughly twenty years later when she again was heard in Court in the same case her memory has cleared and she remembers perfectly well that she gave the suitcases to Stenbeck and Ohlsén. Through my research I have discovered that Miss Bokman together with lawyer Ohlsén signed an inventory list dated 18th and 21st of March 1932.

(0581)

It is very likely that the suitcases contained—at least a part of—the material of evidence that Kreuger had brought with him from America. A considerable amount was probably burned in Paris but it is possible that everything was taken care of by Messrs. Stenbeck and Ohlsén. These documents must have been extremely valuable.

Why would Ivar Krueger's private documents be so important?
Because they contained:

Information about the Italian Bonds; correspondence between the Italian Minister of Finance and IK; and a private letter from Mussolini, with thanks for the help.

Correspondence and documents from New York giving information about the financial interests and persons that were attacking Kreuger.

A list of all Kreuger's contacts and agents which included politicians, diplomats and persons that secretly worked for Kreuger and with whom he had had deposited considerable assets.

(2126)

The same day—the 18th of March—Kreuger's relatives were outmaneuvered from the position as administrators of Ivar Kreuger's estate. From the beginning the estate was going to be taken care of by Torsten Kreuger (Ivar's brother), Gunnar Ekström (Ivar's brother in law) and the lawyer Eliel Löfgren. After some legal footwork, Eliel Löfgren alone became the administrator.

The 18th of March was also the day, when the "investigators"—that sometimes were called "The Royal Commission"—at a meeting with the Board of Directors of Kreuger & Toll decided that the Board no longer could make decisions of their own and that all employees were dismissed.

It is important to observe that at this time the chairman of the commission Torsten Nothin was absent and did not return to Stockholm until March 23rd and did not meet with the other members of the commission until March 24th. In reality this means that it is questionable if the commission as such was formed, and formed a quorum. The only mandate that the commission ever got was to assist the board of directors in their work. A mandate, which they had obviously already exceeded.

3.19.32
On the 19th of March 1932 you could read the following headlines in the two principal Swedish Newspapers.
Svenska Dagbladet
"Three brokers in Paris arrested for baisse actions against Kreuger
Sold collateralized Kreuger securities for 30 million Franc"

(The article is about the broker Barrault. The same name as Kreuger's housekeeper).

In order to free himself he had turned over obviously forged documents to the judge. This morning at ten o'clock Barrault was arrested when he left his home. The police have also arrested two other persons for being involved in the crime in that they had financed Barrault with large sums. As far as TT (Swedish news agency) has been able to gather Barrault was only a tool for large baisse-interests. For the time being it has not been possible to obtain any additional or more detailed information in this particular case.

Dagens Nyheter
(Identical article)

The question is, if this was only the top of an iceberg? Did the part that you could not see or could not obtain any information about have tentacles to Sweden? Involving large financial interests? We know and have shown that some banks and private bankers most likely sold collateral. What would happen if this was revealed? What would have happened if the evidence which Ivar Kreuger brought back from the US were to be made official? The evidence led to some long prison sentences for some French and American brokers. The future development of the case in Sweden was nothing less than remarkable. Powerful Swedish interests arranged for a thick fog to envelop the whole affair. No further investigations were made and no questions were asked. As far as I know no interesting information has ever turned up or been heard of in this matter.

March 28th 1932

In the Swedish police archives I found a note showing that Mr. Stenbeck's partner Ohlsén wrote a memorandum regarding the "Italian Bonds" and made statements about things that he had no possibilities to know anything about. He declared that most probably no agreement regarding monopoly for matches in Italy had ever been made. This, he had been able to determine, within the time of roughly two weeks after the death of Ivar Kreuger. We know that Kreuger had kept the negotiations with Italy very secret. We also know that at the end of March, a board meeting was going to be held in Italy, where the question of a monopoly was going to be settled and in fact was settled. The Kreuger Group held the majority in the Italian match company, that got the monopoly for matches retroactively from the first of January 1932.

4.11.1932

On the 11th of April 1932 the chairman for the investigator commission, Torsten Nothin, made the following note in his diary:

"The 11th of April 1932. During a discussion in Johannes Hellner's room, he offered to go to Italy in order to investigate the Italian Bonds and he also talked about a Spanish transaction that ought to be looked into. At 2.50p.m. Stenbeck was requested to instruct Hellner in all relevant issues."

This note is of extraordinary interest. Not only because it has been recovered from the police archives, but because it shows that it is Hellner that volunteers to go to Italy and possibly also to Spain. This is not the way the story has been described by earlier writers. This nice but weak man, Johannes Hellner, should have volunteered to go to Italy based on instructions given by Hugo Stenbeck. It does sound quite interesting. First of all, Hellner was not a member of the commission and should not know anything about the affairs of Kreuger & Toll and even less about business that Kreuger had wanted to keep secret. As a member of the board of directors in Stockholms Enskilda Bank, Hellner must have been advised by Marcus Wallenberg or Jacob Wallenberg. This is also at a very early stage of the so-called investigation when nothing has been made official about any transactions in Spain. Where did all these details come from?

As for the briefing by Hugo Stenbeck it is quite clear that Johannes Hellner only got the information that Stenbeck wanted him to have and that would tally with the memorandum made by Ohlsén which concluded that K&T did not have any investments at all in Italy. Later this had to be changed, when it was too late, and the damage had already been done.

4.21.32

An extract from Frisk's correspondence with Thor Carlander

"La Liberté yesterday began a series of articles about the Kreuger affair that will continue until their silence is bought."

4.25.1932

Extract from the memoir of the chief of the Criminal Investigation Department, Alvar Zetterquist, 1930-1955.

"When the Government appointed investigation committee (note that the Government never appointed any committee), was informed that Rydbeck planned to go to Paris where his presence was thought to be necessary at a conference with Kreuger interests from the whole world, we got a hint of what was going to happen."

"I finally decided to interrogate Rydbeck at some other place than the office of the police, and chose Ivar Kreuger's own headquarter. Surely this was the first and probably also the last time that the Match Palace lent a room for police interrogation."

"I arranged with Rydbeck that we should meet in the morning in one of the rooms in the Match Palace where I appeared punctually, together with superintendent I R Erlandsson, as witness. Rydbeck had arrived, ahead of us.

The Italian Bonds

"This surprising exposure was made by the investigator that had been appointed by the Government (see above), a week or so before I heard Rydbeck."

—

"When Kreuger returned to Paris from New York and met Rydbeck at his hotel between four and six o'clock (note that. the time is very important) in the afternoon of March 11th 1932—the day before Ivar Kreuger's death—Rydbeck once more raised the question if it was possible to exploit the Italian bonds"

—

"According to information Kreuger had promised not to mortgage or sell the bonds."

A suspicious banker

"Then he told me about an episode from his work together with Ivar Kreuger which to a high degree seemed the bear the stamp of authenticity. Some time during the fall of 1931 Rydbeck had been called to a conference in Amsterdam together with parties interested in the Kreuger Group. It was mainly bankers and representatives from banking institutions in New York, London, Paris, Berlin, Brussels, Luxembourg and some other cities. A Dutch banker with vital interests in various companies in the Kreuger Group was calling the others together. He was well known for his carefulness and rigorous demand for full and satisfactory securities in connection with all granting of credits. At this time he had become worried about the Group's financial standing against the background of the deteriorating business activities of the world market. He had called together the conference in order to give Ivar Kreuger the possibility to personally account for the present situation.

Kreuger had also appeared at the meeting, which took a whole day with only a break for lunch. The Dutch banker had, ahead of time, made a whole list of questions regarding the Group's financial condition and he wanted answers to these questions. He was extremely suspicious of many of Kreuger's larger transactions, and was attacking him in a very inquisitive way.

However, Rydbeck continued, it was amazing to find with what ease Ivar Kreuger could give a reply to each and every question and how convincing his replies seemed to be to all the members of the conference. But the replies were not accepted right off. All the information that Kreuger gave was immediately checked via telephone with respective home offices in New York, London and Paris. Not on one single point was it possible to show that Kreuger had given incorrect information.

The Dutch banker, who also had been elected chairman, ended the conference by thanking Kreuger for all the information he had given and he declared: "Yes, I thought that the Group's financial position was good after all. But I had not expected that it was that good."

—

"Even if you considered the Italian securities to be without any value it would be possible, through a careful liquidation of the bankruptcy, to save and preserve such large values that a reconstruction of the concern would not be unthinkable, said Rydbeck."

"At the same time he expressed certain fears for the hostile feelings against Ivar Kreuger that you could find among many influential people some of them among the American financial institutions. He believed that the psychosis in connection with Kreuger's sudden death could jeopardize all sensible attempts to reconstruct the Group."

It is important to note that the above mentioned conference was held roughly six months prior to Ivar Kreuger's death. Was the Swedish investigator committee really so smart that they in less than two weeks could determine that the Kreuger Group was ready for bankruptcy? In fact were these non-businessmen more knowledgeable than all the above mentioned bankers from all over Europe and America?

The Murder of Ivar Kreuger

In November 1931 Mr. Henning had met Kreuger in Berlin. At this time Kreuger had seemed very optimistic and shown a consolidated balance sheet for the Swedish and Dutch Kreuger & Toll. Mr. Henning had made certain remarks about this and based on that Kreuger had suggested that Henning, Holm and Wendler together should examine the financial books of the whole Kreuger group. (Henning, Holm and Wendler were accountants).

Within a period of roughly 6 months we have the following rather interesting incidents. Kreuger asks three of his accountants to make an examination of the Groups financial accounts. He makes a presentation of the Groups affairs at a conference with international bankers. When in America he asks his American banker to arrange with an independent firm of accountants to examine the Group's international business. This was confirmed on March 23rd in a record from a meeting with the board of directors of Kreuger & Toll. You must ask the question: Is this what you do if you know that your company books are not in order? Or is this what you do if you are convinced that your Group will come out greatly strengthened after such an examination of financial records, at the same time as you can present clear evidence against those that have been "lending" of the concern's assets in order to "help" the short sellers that were in trouble? It was a good idea to be able to compare the results of the analysis of the group's finances, by several different auditors from different nationalities. Not many groups were as extensive (or powerful) and an agreement among such auditors, of the "Empire's" stability, could have removed several opponents.

6.15.32
Extract from a letter from Frisk to Dardel.

"Banque de Suéde wants to borrow 30 million francs against a first mortgage on the real estate at Place Vendome. The costs have been 115 million and it requires another 10 million in order to finish construction. Remaining 20 million needed to strengthen and secure the bank. Place Vendome was given firm on hand to a Mr. Rosenthal, a broker in Paris.

The accountants that were called in by the investigator committee had been ordered to keep away from certain assets such as the French and German real estate and Deutsche Union Bank and a few others. These special assets were to be managed in many, crooked ways so that they finally could be transferred to those companies in the Group that had been taken over by the new owners.

9.17.32
Extract from a letter by Mr. H Ashton

"A long time might pass and the feelings could be completely different, before this case will be brought up in the High Court. You can already note a definite change in the press. Maybe Kreuger will once more become the hero and Sandstrom (the prosecutor) the ruffian.

If there, as Ashton writes, were a general change of the feelings, it quickly changed. This is difficult to understand today, but in 1932 very many people were afraid.

12.31.1933 Berth
Extract from a letter from Dardel in Geneva to Frisk
    "Just bought a company from the bankruptcy estate of Kreuger & Toll which will give us a profit of 100-200,000".

"Shares in one company owned by Kreuger & Toll were dumped by the liquidators. They never bothered to look into the "hidden reserves". For example Allgemeine Finansgesellschaft had a hidden reserve of Swiss Fr. 500,000 from the liquidation of Brupbacher".

"Dardel informs that Brupbacher's liquidation remitted Swiss Fr. 22,119:50 but that he had no intention to inform Kreuger & Toll about this."

What is noted above are just a few examples showing quality of knowledge of international business and banking that the managers of Kreuger & Toll's estate had. Probably they did not even know what "hidden reserves" were. The question is if not large parts of the Kreuger Group were managed in the same way. The buyers who knew the real value made good deals, while owners of debentures and shares lost large amounts on account of the managers lack of knowledge and interest, and concern.

11.2.1934
Extract from Ashton to Frisk.
"International Match 13 5/8 and Kreuger bonds 25-25 1/2. Jacob Wallenberg went to New York in order to arrange a meeting in London regarding the way of payment/settlement between Germany and England. He was very positive regarding International Match and Kreuger bonds. Berth has a part in the account "Trio" in Intern.Match/Englander/Lichtensteiges. We are Ernst Englander, Hirch Lilienthal & Co and Berth."

The letter is dated at the end of 1934 and it shows that there is a positive feeling for International Match as well as Kreuger bonds. It also shows that some sort of consortium has been formed in order to invest in these securities. In other words, Kreuger securities were not all that bad.

Below are a few comments about the economy/estates of some of the people that were acting in connection with the estates of Kreuger & Toll and Ivar Kreuger.

The Economy of some of the main actors in the Krueger case

1931 This was the last year that IK declared income	Salary as management director in STAB		120,000
	Salary as Director on duty in Stockholms Intecknings Garanti AB. Tantiem (remuneration)		10,000 24,053:97
	Board of Directors—Grängesberg Tantiem		7,000 6,997:50
	Board of directors Ryl. & Aspl.		1, 000
	Board of directors K&T		4, 000
	Dividends		6, 034, 188
	Taxed value of real estate		109, 500
	Securities		101,327, 455
	Claims		26,759,038
	Other assets		962, 500
	Total assets	129,580,493	
	Total debts	92,713,493	
	Net result	36,445,000	

The declaration was at that time—just as it is to day—the basis for the calculation of income and wealth taxes. I believe that Ivar Kreuger only showed what he had to show—just as people do to day.

A couple of very clever lawyers worked for some time with Ivar Kreuger's income situation and managed to come up with a very large negative result.

The same year—1931—the lawyer Hugo Stenbeck declared assets for 59,070:—, income from capital 1,730:—and paid taxes of 5,567:79

The first of the "investigators" that died—in 1938—was Hugo Stenbeck's partner Olle Ohlsén. Their law firm made the declaration for his estate. The assets amounted to 184,434:—and the cost of de declaration amounted to 500:-. Hugo Stenbeck elected the lawyer Folke Rogard to represent Ohlsén's daughter. Folke Rogard owed Kreuger & Toll 100,000 against collateral but got debt reduced to 60,000. Rogard was also the lawyer who was elected to the position of CEO of the company Hogbroforsen, just in order to be able to declare it in bankruptcy.

Professor Martin Fehr, a member of the investigators committee as well as of the management commission, also died in 1938 leaving an estate of 338,718:-

In 1940 the lawyer Eliel Löfgren died leaving an estate of 167,568:—with a cost of 145:—for the declaration. Eliel Löfgren had been "taking care of" Ivar Kreuger's estate. He went to Paris in order to "assist" the banker A V Hogman to arrange a deal with the French consortium that had been speculating against Ivar Kreuger and Kreuger & Toll, with among other things forged documents.

In 1943 Marcus Wallenberg sr. died leaving an estate of 9,793,782:66. The cost of the declaration 25,000:-.

In 1945 Carl Frisk died, leaving an estate of 372,540:—after having arranged with gifts for the family of 2,400,000:-. The cost of the declaration was 5,000:-.

In 1945 Nils Edén also died leaving an estate of 158,183:-

In 1947 Johannes Hellner died leaving an estate of 364,965:—at a cost of 4,000:-

In 1949 Josef Sachs died leaving an estate of 249,433:-

In 1951 the lawyer Tom Forssner died leaving an estate of 236,370:—at a cost of 1,000:-

In 1971 Marc Wallenberg died leaving an estate of 10,638,349:—at a cost of 60,000:-

In 1973 the lawyer Folke Rogard died leaving an estate of 135,900:—at a cost of 6,000:-

In 1974 Rolf Calissendorf died leaving an estate of 1,151,417:—at a cost of 5,428:-

In 1976 the lawyer Hugo Stenbeck Jr. died leaving an estate of 11,554,434:—at a cost of 161,000:-.

In 1977 the lawyer Hugo Stenbeck Sr. died leaving an estate of 8,933,663:—at a cost of 131,000.

In 1980 Jacob Wallenberg died leaving an estate of 81,785,007:—at a cost of 107,664:-

In 1982 Sune Schéle died leaving an estate of 766,642:—(after gifts of some real estate to the family) at a cost of 10,000:-

In 1982 Ernfrid Browaldh also died leaving an estate of 2,516,169:—at a cost of 20,600:-.

In 1982 Marcus Wallenberg jr. died leaving an estate of 66,836,943:—at a cost of 102,922:-.

In 1992 Märta Stenbeck died, the wife of the lawyer Hugo Stenbeck sr., leaving an estate of 87,232,101:—(+ approx. 27,500,000 due to lower rates of taxation for certain stocks) at a cost of 323,000:-.

The estate declaration documents after a deceased person is an interesting reading if you read them in a correct way. They do not only give you information about the deceased and his/her economy but also about the whole family and how their economy has been planned and how the assets have been divided within the family. The Swedish estate declaration is an official document. The information that I will use here, is such that I believe that they might possibly have something to do with the contents of this book, directly or indirectly and in some cases a little bit peripheral.

From the time of Ivar Kreuger's death, in 1932, until the last death of the persons in the list above, in 1992, sixty years have passed. During these years there has been one world war and we have lived through several periods of inflation of various intensities. Therefore, it is impossible to compare the figures right off.

There were two bank directors—Ernfrid Browaldh and Jacob Wallenberg—in the investigators committee. There is a large difference between Browaldh's assets of 2,516,169 and Wallenberg's assets of 81,785,007. This depends to a certain extent on the fact that Wallenberg got a foundation through inheritance, but the difference is never the less remarkable. The two gentlemen had different views of the economy in general. Practically all of Browaldh's assets were in the form of premium bonds—a rather passive investment—while Wallenberg's consisted of a mixture of stocks and bonds. In fact some of the German Government 4% bonds from 1930, called the Match Loan, were declared at 94% of the face value.

None of the lawyers that I have studied and that had any part in the Kreuger investigation have had an estate with an unusually large fortune. With one exception—Hugo Stenbeck—where the estate showed a balance of 8,933,663. This sum should however be adjusted, with a sum of roughly 46 million, which previously was set aside.

It can be established that the two families that one way or the other were involved in the administration and winding up of the estates of Kreuger & Toll and Ivar Kreuger have become very rich. Hugo Stenbeck had his law firm and Wallenberg's their inheritance and their bank but what they could manage to extract from their respective businesses in form of salaries and bonuses could not, after taxes, explain the capital that has been amassed and declared. It is true that these gentlemen were extremely skillful, each one within his special field. Investments on the Stock Exchange can explain parts of their fortune but stocks have a tendency to move up as well as down.

Looking at their declarations of estate you find that they have one thing in common. Debts! There are considerable amounts of loans. If you have a bank you also have cheap access to money and with a well-known law firm you do not seem to have any difficulties either.

A declaration of estate, consist of a specification over the assets of the deceased. Normally this is not a problem; neither does it require too much time. However, if you have to do extensive investigations, redistributions and other transactions, with or within the assets of the estate, in order to be able to hide or at least not account for everything, then the fees increase. For this reason I included the fees the respective families had to pay. The cost for the estates of four members of the Wallenberg family—where Marcus Wallenberg, Sr. is the first one—amounts to a total sum of 295,586:—The declarations have been made by Stockholms Enskilda Bank (controlled by the family).

The cost for the estates of three members of the Stenbeck family (Jan Stenbeck not included) amounts to a total sum of 615.000:—The declarations have been made by their own law-firm.

It is up to you to read these figures any way you like it.

BOGOVOUT

WHO PURCHASED THE PISTOL?

If Ivar Kreuger was at another location, when the weapon was purchased,—who was it that bought the pistol and the ammunition.?

Notes, made by the previously departed Soviet Delegation Advisor Dimitrievskij, have provided information and shed light on how it really could have happened. His writings are interesting in many ways, since they provide the description of the man, who was present in Paris and was seen on several occasions in and around the neighborhood of the building, where Ivar Kreuger had his apartment.

The following are some excerpts from the notes, left behind by Dimitrievskij, in which, a certain Vladimir Petrovitsj Bogovout Kolomistaev is described.

"B came from a high class and rich, noble Ukranian family and had received the best education. When Shoropadskijst formed his government in 1918 in the Ukrain, he was a participant. His father-in-law was the minister of labor. Bogovout showed a capability for handling risky financial exchange business matters, etc. He emigrated to Konstantinopel, where he came in contact with soviet underground agents, during the years of 1921-1922. He then began to work with them in the areas of politics and economy. He demonstrated great capabillities, in the wining over of some patriarchs of the Greek-Orthodox Church, through the use of subsidies and support. He was requested to travel to Moscow to make a report of his work, which presentation greatly impressed the GPU (the political police) management, especially its chief, Dserjinskij. After this, he was again sent abroad on various delicate missions, to London, Paris, and others. His main job was to contact people, in important positions in the areas of finance, industry, etc., but he was mainly an agent in the Soviet Secret Service."

"In spite of the semi-darkness, I could see him (B) quite well and it struck me that his oval face, the shape of his head, yes, through his entire carriage—he had something, which made him look like Ivar Kreuger. Even my wife was amazed of this likeness. Even his slow and methodical voice, was reminiscent of IK. In conversations he gave the impression of being a business man and politician."

169

"Even in full lighting in Hotel Regina, one was amazed from his behavior, which showed a certain ill defined likeness of IK—mostly in his carriage. Especially, when he came into a room, moved around the same and began to speak on a first name basis, did he show this likeness. Later—in conversations—this likeness disappeared, only to reappear, when he showed up the next time."

"After IK's death, I began to analyze this story and then I started to realize that Bogovout, possibly could have played a part in the matter. First and most importantly, I came to the conclusion that it could have been he who bought the revolver (the pistol—my notes). On a quick visit, he could have caused people, who did not know Ivar Kreuger, to think that he was Ivar. After the occupation of France, the Germans started investigations of IK's death. Their results showed that he was murdered. They also indicated that the murder had been done on the initiatives of Soviet and certain American family circles. They also firmly established that *it was Bogovout, who bought the murder weapon*. I was informed of all this, privately—it was known that I was interested in the matter."

"I also heard that the Germans did not count Bogovout as a murderer, but as a collaborating intermediary. I also had the feeling that Bogovout was not able to kill somebody, through shooting. He was more of a poison mixer type. He could use poison. He could also bring the murderer into IK's house. After IK's death, Bogovout was scared, tremendously scared. He was, at that time, working with the GPU—resident for Europe, Goldstein (Berlin) and the resident in Paris, Istgushkij."

"Furthermore, Bogovout had connections with the head of a bank in Paris, Navasina, which cooperated with Enskilda Banken and with the managing director of a Russian bank, Trepjakov, in Paris. I have all reasons for suspecting that he also worked for the house of Morgan. Ivar Kreuger was, during his entire trip from New York to Paris, under constant surveillance and in the attack against him, certain members of the French Police assisted."
NSDK2671-2675

This is what we know from Dimitrievskij's notes. There were other connections to Bogovout as well. In the Price and Waterhouse report from their examination of the company France-Afrique SA, there are descriptions of how funds were moved to Italy, amongst other countries, for the acquisition of match factories in these. An amount of S.Kr. 209,411.60 appears in the books, as payment to Bogovout and his assistant, Rachkovitch. Paul L. Rachkovitch was a former match manufacturer in Soviet Union.
IK8255

Bogovout also plays a certain roll in the Lessine-business and he had a secret position as the representative of "tjeckans" (now the KGB), in England and France, with possibilities of direct contact with the highest leveled politicians and others.

An interesting question: Is Bogovout that person, who is refered to, by the "B" in Dardel's somewhat cryptical letter of 30 March, 1934 (page 137), which was written by order of the District Judge Wallenberg?

Epilog

It is not my intention to cover what happened in Sweden and/or in other parts of the world after the death of Ivar Kreuger in this book. That will come later. The important thing for me has been to show the likelihood that Ivar Kreuger was murdered. His opponents have had ample time and funds to enable them to remove and/or change documents and other types of evidence. This has of course made it possible for them to maintain whatever they want. It has also made research quite difficult as you are trying to complete a puzzle where you suddenly find one or another part missing. The opponents of Ivar Kreuger changed history. I hope to see it changed once more.

—

Dr Sven Olof Arleback wrote a book about the Kreuger crash in which he points out that the banks, Handelsbanken and the Wallenberg's sphere, are those that gained the most from the crash. I feel that a few extracts—freely translated—from Mr. Arleback's book will support what I have stated above.

"Page 181: There are reasons to believe that the material in the archive has been manipulated in order to suit the opponents and the way they account for their actions. It is also possible to prove that some documents actually are missing in the archive.

Page 178: There was hardly any swindle behind the economy of Kreuger & Toll from the part of Ivar Kreuger. Not even the statements that the "Italian bonds" had been used have been proven correct; in any case not in the books of Kreuger & Toll.

—

It is more likely that Ivar Kreuger himself was swindled rather than that he was swindling other people. But also his pronounced kindness caused him large losses.

—

It was therefore that Handelsbanken and the Wallenberg sphere, gained the most from the bankruptcy of Kreuger & Toll (Jacob Wallenberg with insider position made considerable speculations in the shares of STAB).

The Murder of Ivar Kreuger

Of course it could not be deliberate that Government Bonds to the value of SEK 400 Million and shares for close to SEK100 Million were omitted? Could it? If these blocks had been accounted for the bankruptcy would have been impossible."

—

Many times I have been asked who it was within the Kreuger Group that worked against Kreuger and gave and lent information as well as securities to opponents or competitors. I am going to mention something about the lines that I am working on, collecting pieces of evidence and information in order to, finally be able to present a case. At present there is no unambiguous evidence. That is of course the nature of a case like this but there are circumstantial evidences, some strong, some not so strong and some weak. But by adding them together you get a chain, in fact a rather long and also durable chain.

The person or persons you are looking for must have had such a position that the access to the Group's securities and internal information has been limitless. Erik Sjostrom, Gunnar Bergenstrahle and Sune Schéle belonged, at least during the last few years, to this category and they have not been able to account for where substantial amounts of debentures and other securities disappeared.

I have followed Bergenstråhle, and as previously mentioned Oscar Rydbeck noted that Ivar Kreuger reacted negatively, when he was informed that Bergenstrahle had come to Paris. There is actually no explanation at all why he came. Bergenstrahle was chief for the Investment Department of Kreuger & Toll, a position that gave him unlimited access to all debentures and shares that the concern or Ivar Kreuger had at their disposal. I have found that receipts and journals from the Investment Department do not tally (RA). It could be that the evidence that Kreuger carried with him when he returned from the USA, held evidence about debentures and shares that had been put on the market without the consent of Kreuger. It was Bergenstråhle's responsibility to ensure that such things would not happen. It is quite possible that Kreuger had discovered that the journals did not tally with presented records. In any case, Kreuger did not seem to be very satisfied with Bergenstrahle in March 1932.

There are a few other remarkable things in connection with Bergenstrahle that I mentioned in my first book so I will not repeat them here. To these can however be added that Bergenstrahle is one of the very few, considering the position that he had, that was not bothered by the police or was brought to Court. He quickly obtained a new position within the Wallenberg controlled companies and was a member of the Board in Deutsche Union Bank. Wallenberg declared, after having taken care of the stocks, that the value for this bank was Zero. It seems that Bergenstråhle was needed on the Board, as he held that position until 1945. My research at the Riksarkivet

173

revealed that all communications from Kreuger & Toll, as well as Ivar Kreuger's private communications, passed through the Investment Department. Today such information could be filtered. This might explain why Wallenberg's from time to time, seemed to have reliable inside information from the Kreuger Group.

Many things remain to be researched in order to fully resolve what happened. Who, for example, represented Ivar Kreuger's and Kreuger & Tolls shares in Deutsche Union Bank? Who represented the Group's interest in connection with the sale of the unaccounted shares in the Italian companies? The companies that Hugo Stenbeck claimed did not exist—but that still exist? What happened to the real estate in various countries? How were the wind-ups of the various estates handled? What happened to all the foreign holdings and how were they accounted for—and by whom? What fortunes were created by the fall of the Kreuger Group? For who was more than 700,000 debentures bought the weeks after Krueger's death? During my work with this book I have assembled more than 5,000 documents—copies of which are kept in the US. These documents will help me to show how the Kreuger Empire was torn apart and plundered.

I will end this book by repeating the words of Doctor Olle Lindquist:

"Those who arranged with the inhibition of the autopsy *against* the advice from the French police doctor, *against* the advice from two of the top specialist on forensic medicine in Sweden and *against* the wish of the family must have had very weighty reasons—otherwise you do not do a thing like this."

Printed in the United States
149003LV00003B/149/P